Vivaria
Designs

FROM THE EXPERTS AT
ADVANCED VIVARIUM SYSTEMS™

By Jerry G. Walls

THE HERPETOCULTURAL LIBRARY™
Advanced Vivarium Systems™
Irvine, California

Karla Austin, *Business Operations Manager*
Nick Clemente, *Special Consultant*
Barbara Kimmel, *Managing Editor*
Jessica Knott, *Production Supervisor*
Honey Winters, *Designer*
Design concept by Michael Vincent Capozzi
Indexed by Melody Englund

Photographs by Paul Freed.

LCCN: 96-183295
ISBN: 1-882770-92-7

An Imprint of BowTie Press®
A Division of BowTie, Inc.
3 Burroughs
Irvine, CA 92618
866-888-5526

Printed and bound in Singapore
10 9 8 7 6 5 4 3 2 1

CONTENTS

Introduction 4

1 The Cage Really Matters 5

2 Substrates 25

3 Landscaping and Decorations 38

4 Lighting and Heating a Vivarium 63

5 Tools for the Herp Keeper 79

6 Woodland Vivaria .91

7 Rain Forest Vivaria 95

8 Desert Vivaria 100

9 Wet Vivaria 108

10 Outdoor Vivaria 115

11 Sterile Vivaria .133

Resources 139

Index 140

About the Author .144

INTRODUCTION

Keeping reptiles and amphibians in glass boxes—vivaria or terraria—is a hobby that has been popular for almost two centuries in Europe and the United States. Early German and British hobbyists developed the basics of how we keep reptiles and amphibians today. Some say that the hobby reached its peak with the work of the German naturalist Willy Wolterstorff (1864–1943), who succeeded in keeping and breeding delicate newts and other salamanders that even today are considered tough or nearly impossible to keep.

However, the modern vivarium hobby is changing rapidly, with new materials and new methods becoming available at a stunning pace. In my opinion, there has never been a better time to keep a vivarium. Now even a beginner can succeed without years of experience.

In this book, I'll talk about the many types of containers and substrates available and discuss ways of lighting and heating a vivarium that our predecessors could only dream of just a few decades ago. After you read this book, you will be able to find your way through the equipment section of a pet shop and recognize the equipment that best fits your needs. You also will develop an idea of which equipment is really necessary and which is a luxury.

Although this is not a book about vivarium animals, there should be enough examples mentioned of commonly kept amphibians and reptiles for you to handle most species found in pet shops. I've included an introduction to outdoor cages for turtles and tortoises or chameleons and large lizards.

For the material in this book, I'm indebted to the works of such modern vivarium masters as Philippe de Vosjoli, R. D. Bartlett, and Rex Lee Searcey as well as earlier workers such as Willy Wolterstorff and Elke Zimmermann.

CHAPTER 1

THE CAGE REALLY MATTERS

The proper way to set up a vivarium—the cage in which your nonaquatic reptile or amphibian pet will spend its life—has long been a controversial but essential topic in the herpetocultural hobby. There is no single correct way to keep any reptile or amphibian (called herps for short). There are many ways that work and some that don't. Each way has its advantages and problems, its advocates and detractors. The goal of this book is to give you an idea of the numerous ways you can set up a vivarium and the commonly available products you can use. The book covers cages, heating and lighting, substrates (bedding), and some of the equipment you will find useful.

There are too many species of herps from too many different habitats to give exact plans for building vivaria for every particular type of herp. Instead, this book will provide

Vivaria can range from elaborate naturalistic setups, such as this one, to basic sterile setups.

good, general ideas on how to make a habitat for your pet, focusing on a few basic types of environments and a few common herps. For specific instructions on creating a suitable environment for your herp, consult a book about that species.

A gentle reminder: herps do not do well in cardboard boxes or plastic bags. Before buying your pet, set up its cage correctly, with the right lighting and heating to meet its needs. Know that you can buy essential foods locally and reliably. If you don't have a local source for food, start breeding your own food before purchasing a pet. Many of the common food animals, such as crickets, mealworms, superworms, and even mice, can be cultured at home at little cost. Starter cultures of many of these are available from advertisers in *Reptiles* magazine and over the Internet. More herps are probably lost in the first month of ownership than at any other time. A new owner may be enthused about the animal but negligent of its environment. Get the cage completed and food ready before you buy that pet lizard or snake.

Types of Cages

There are several types of cages, including aquariums, tubs, and snake drawer units. The type of cage you select will depend on your specific pets and interests. It also will

Vivarium vs. Terrarium vs. Aquarium

What is the difference between a vivarium and a terrarium? A terrarium is an enclosure used to raise plants and sometimes small animals. A vivarium is an enclosure used to house small animals (although it may contain plants). In herpetoculture, the term *vivarium* is the one most commonly used. An aquarium is an enclosure with water used to house aquatic plants and small animals.

depend to some extent on your budget and how deeply you plan to go into keeping your animals. If you plan to keep just one or two pets, then you probably will be willing to spend more money and time on a decorative vivarium that shows off your pets. If breeding is your major plan, then you will look more closely at cages that allow you to keep many animals efficiently in minimal space.

Types of Vivaria

There are five basic types of simple vivaria for use with amphibians and reptiles. These types include:

- Sterile: used for temporary housing, hospital cages, or quarantine confinement. Often used in laboratories as well.

- Wet: used for many amphibians and quite a few small lizards and some turtles. A wet vivarium is used for any animal that needs lots of humidity at all times and moist bedding. The wet vivarium merges into the aquarium, especially if there is more water than there is land.

- Rain Forest: a high-humidity, warm vivarium usually set up for arboreal (tree-dwelling) lizards and snakes as well as for specialized tropical tree frogs. A rain forest vivarium is usually taller than it is wide to accommodate branches.

- Woodland: the basic, middle-of-the-line vivarium useful for almost all common snakes and lizards as well as some turtles.

- Desert: used for lizards and desert snakes that require very dry, hot conditions.

The Aquarium

An aquarium is basically a glass-sided box meant to hold water and, usually, fish. However, it long has been the most available cage for a great variety of herps, and it still has many advantages. An aquarium is easy to purchase almost anywhere and usually is quite affordable. Today, you can even find aquariums specially designed for herps that live on mossy substrates. These aquariums have thinner glass than those designed for fish. They may even be marked "Not designed to hold water." Aquariums are usually all glass, with four sides, a bottom, and a lid. The bottom is made of

Aquarium tanks come in many different sizes. Which one you need depends on the type of animal you have and the number.

strong glass bonded with silicone cement for a long life and easy maintenance.

An aquarium is a decent to excellent cage for many types of salamanders, such as spotted salamanders (*Ambystoma maculatum*) and the woodland salamanders (*Desmognathus* spp. and *Plethodon* spp., for instance), which need moist surroundings including live mosses and soil. Aquariums also work well for many types of frogs (including poison frogs), turtles, lizards, and snakes, as long as they do not need lots of vertical space or ventilation.

Many amphibians and smaller reptiles can be kept in a 20-gallon (76-liter) aquarium, which will house two or three of almost any frog, salamander, small ground-dwelling lizard, or small snake. Turtles, however, generally should not be crowded into a tank even when small because they produce a large amount of waste. A 20-gallon (76-liter) aquarium can easily house an adult corn snake (*Elaphe guttata*) or similarly inactive snakes that are less than 4 feet (122 cm) in length.

Aquariums are convenient for young animals, such as hatchling iguanas. You will probably find, however, that within a year most iguanas will grow too large to maintain in a regular aquarium. For iguanas and other large lizards and snakes, you should invest in special cages as soon as the animal starts growing—which will be within a few months of purchase.

Aquariums are easy to clean. It is easy to sanitize an aquarium by removing everything and just soaking the tank down with a 10 percent or better solution of household bleach and then fully rinsing it with running water. Aquariums come in many sizes, available from 2 ½ to 110 gallons (9.5 to 418 liters) and more. They also come in different shapes and proportions. The common 20-gallon (76-liter) tank, for instance, usually is 12 inches (30 cm) high and 24 inches (61 cm) long, but a "high 20" is 16 inches (40 cm) high, and a "long 20" is 30 inches (76 cm) long. Aquariums of much over 20 gallons (76 liters), which are about 30 inches long and 12 inches high and wide (76 x 30 x 30 cm) in the long form, do best when on their own stands, which can be expensive. Always try to buy an aquarium that is a standard size because fittings such as lids are made only in certain sizes. It can be incredibly annoying having half a dozen usable aquariums but no decent lids.

There are problems with aquariums. They are heavy if they have more than a 30-gallon (114-liters) capacity. They are rarely tall enough to be used satisfactorily with animals that need extensive basking areas (such as larger lizards) requiring a heat lamp placed over the top of the aquarium. Aquariums do not provide enough ventilation for delicate herps such as chameleons. It also can be very hard to reach into the corners to clean them fully.

Lids

An aquarium without a lid is almost worthless. Always buy a lid when you buy an aquarium, and keep the two together. The typical lid is a single piece that has to be lifted off the aquarium to open the tank. Some lids have a

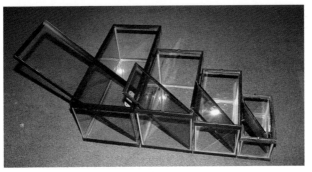

Lids such as the ones shown here are indispensable parts of all vivaria. Choose one that will meet the specific needs of your herp.

long hinge near the center, allowing you to lift just part of the lid to put in food or water and reduce the chances of fast-moving frogs or lizards escaping. Some manufacturers sell an interesting frame that fits snugly on the aquarium and has a mesh or perforated metal plate that slides in grooves to allow access to the tank. Although expensive, these are excellent lids.

If you are going to keep a snake, lizard, or turtle that needs a basking light, you need a lid that has a steel frame and heavy quarter-inch mesh wire. Lids made with plastic frames and fiberglass window-screen mesh will warp or even burn if a basking light is placed on them. It is only a matter of time before you unthinkingly place a hot light over the frame and turn your back "for a second," only to find melting plastic when you return. Plastic-framed lids can work for frogs and salamanders (which don't need hot lighting), but the lids seldom fit securely enough to the edges of the aquarium to assure that an animal cannot escape.

There are new flexible lids that fasten to the frame of the aquarium with Velcro tabs. These lids might be useful with turtles that don't try to climb to the top of the vivarium, but they may not prevent the escape of a small snake or a determined gecko. Once a snake or a lizard pries its snout into a loose area near the fastening, it can wriggle out and escape.

Modifications to Aquariums

Advanced keepers often modify the aquariums they use by placing a drain in one corner of the floor (so rain can be simulated to convince some frogs to breed) or by increasing ventilation by placing small panels of very fine mesh near the tops of two opposite sides of the aquarium. Glass is a hard material for most of us to work with. It really is difficult to drill in a drain at the bottom or cut holes across two sides of a glass aquarium. Cutting glass calls for special tools and some experience. I have found that many aquariums tend to crack outward from any drilled holes. Be careful.

Some pet supply shops will drill holes and cut glass for you (at a price, of course), and then you can fit appropriate drain or mesh panels into place using silicone cement. You may also be able to find aquariums with drains and additional ventilation slots in the sides already in place.

This hinge clip secures the lid to the vivarium and prevents animals from escaping. Keep an extra hinge clip in case the first breaks or is lost.

Metal lids are almost always best, and they are not much more expensive than plastic lids. If you think the mesh of the lid is too large (baby geckos, for instance, can squeeze through quarter-inch mesh), just cut a piece of window screen to fit. Tape it under the larger mesh of the lid with duct tape. (Duct tape will hold up to a considerable amount of moisture and heat.)

Every time you buy a lid, buy at least two pairs of hinge clips. These are little semicircles of spring steel that wedge under the aquarium frame at one end and on top of the lid frame on the other. Use one pair of clips on opposite short edges of the aquarium, and keep the other pair for backup when the first pair is lost or breaks. If you suspect your pet (generally a larger snake) can lift the unsecured edges of the lid, use a pair of clips on the long edges as well. This is the most simple and practical way to securely attach a lid to an

A keeper drills a hole in the side of this aquarium to improve ventilation. This task requires some expertise, however, to keep from shattering the glass; ask the pet shop or an experienced friend for help.

aquarium. You can also use a special locking latch made to secure a sliding door or window. Piling books or bricks on top of the lid won't work and can lead to serious accidents if the pile falls over and breaks the glass.

Tubs and Shoe Boxes

Any variety store will sell a range of plastic boxes, tubs, and storage containers varying from perhaps a quart (liter) to 10 or 15 gallons (38 or 57 liters). These are the modern equivalents of the old plastic shoe box used for many years for keeping snakes of several types. These plastic containers are great cages for certain types of herps, including those that don't need high security and don't need basking lights. Most of the plastics used to make these containers are not stable at higher temperatures. They seldom are optically clear, which means you can't view your pet through the sides of the container. Instead, you have to look down at your pet. Since corn snakes and their like prefer the dark anyway, this can be an advantage because relatively little light enters from the sides.

A major problem is providing a suitable lid for a container. The lids that come with them seldom fasten securely and are designed to prevent air movement, so ventilation in the container is negligible. You can modify a lid by cutting a hole at least 4 inches (10 cm) wide along the center and then covering the hole from below with mesh of an appropriate

Plastic tubs such as this one are suitable enclosures for pets that do not require basking lights. Unlike glass aquariums, plastic tubs can be easily modified with air holes.

A large plastic tub works well for housing turtles.

size. Fiberglass screen can be held in place by silicone cement and sealers, and quarter-inch metal mesh can be held in place by using short bolts with wide washers and nuts. These are easy even for non–do-it-yourself types.

Very large tubs, such as those used for livestock, water troughs, or koi ponds, work well for turtles. They also work well for spiny-tailed lizards (genus *Uromastyx*) and similar species that are not great climbers. They usually are made of thick, heavy black or blue plastic or rubber and are 50 to 100 or more gallons (190 to 380 liters) in capacity. Typical shapes are rectangles, ovals, and circles. A 50-gallon (190-liter) tub is roughly 3 feet long, 18 inches wide, and 18 to 20 inches high (91 x 46 x 46 to 50 cm), which is large enough to form a permanent home for a smaller turtle, such as a Russian tortoise (*Testudo horsfieldii*), or the winter home for a larger species being kept indoors temporarily. The largest convenient size for indoor use probably is the 110-gallon (418-liter), which is roughly 50 inches long, 32 inches wide, and 20 inches high (127 x 80 x 50 cm)—quite a tub!

To view your animals, you have to look into stock tubs from above. They are deep enough that you can easily build a wooden frame over the tub to hold basking lights at a safe distance from the herp. For semiaquatic turtles, drill a hole the size of a standard plumbing drain in the bottom at one end. Use a stopper (available at hardware stores), and run a

Small (usually less than 10 gallons, 38 liters), clear plastic boxes with flimsy but colorful slotted plastic lids are widely sold in pet supply shops and have their uses in the herp room. They have three major problems:

1. The slots in the lid always break. (For extra security, use fiberglass window screen stretched across the actual top of the box and held in place by the frame of the lid).
2. They quickly discolor and become almost opaque.
3. They warp under even moderate heat.

Never trust the handle on the lid; it often fails at the worst possible time. Although undertank heaters and basking lights are made for these plastic boxes, they are not efficient or trustworthy and are quite expensive. Critter boxes are great temporary containers and work for many baby herps and small invertebrate pets, but they cannot be trusted as permanent cages.

drain tube out of it. This way you can easily change the water and rinse down the tub every other day.

Large stock tubs and koi ponds (which are designed to be placed into the soil) can be used outdoors as well as indoors, but remember that heavy rains could turn them into death traps. Drill several small drain holes in the sides at a level low enough to prevent drowning in case of sudden storms. You will need a lid for many types of herps (turtles are the

This critter box works fine for corn snakes and a few other easy keepers. The weak lid and easily warped material of these boxes, however, make them impractical for most herps.

major exception as few can climb out of a cage). Lids are needed more to keep dogs, cats, and birds out than to keep turtles or lizards in. For a lid, build a wooden frame and cover it with mesh. Secure it in place with at least two sliding latches or with hook and eye screws.

Snake Drawers

One specialty cage that proves very useful if you keep large numbers of snakes such as corn snakes and kingsnakes (*Lampropeltis* spp.) or small boas is one with snake drawers. A snake drawer unit consists of many shallow drawers that slide in and out of a wooden frame. A unit usually holds from eight to twenty shallow drawers. Each drawer fits into its frame tightly enough that no lid is needed for the drawer. Heat is supplied by built-in heating strips under the back end of the drawers in each row.

Keepers with a large number of snakes may opt to keep them in snake drawer units.

This type of cage will hold a surprising number of different snakes, basically any kind that does not need a basking light. They are far from a natural-looking habitat (generally each drawer has a hide box, a water bowl, and a layer of aspen), but they certainly are efficient if you are breeding kingsnakes, for instance, and need lots of room as the young grow up. Commonly, mating pairs are kept in a unit with a few larger drawers, and babies are kept in a unit with many small drawers.

On the downside, it is hard to keep a constant temperature over the unit or to modify the heating strips to make some drawers warmer than others. Additionally, the particle board from which most snake drawer units are made is very heavy and absorbs water easily. This makes moving and cleaning the framework difficult.

Laboratory Cages

All of the cages discussed above open from the top. This means you must reach in from the top to get to the animal. However, there are many cages that open from the front instead. These use one or two sheets of tempered glass or Plexiglas across the front. The glass slides back in rails or grooves to allow access. Originally designed for use in biology laboratories, these generally are expensive cages. However, they are among the best designs for snakes and lizards.

Such cages are not good choices for moisture-loving amphibians; it is hard to keep wet bedding inside (it falls out the front when the glass slides back). The same is true of desert-loving herps because the sand bedding will fall out. You can try adding a strip of plastic or aluminum to form an extra-tall lip along the bottom edge behind the glass to prevent this.

Laboratory cages come in many varieties, but most are made of fiberglass or a heavy molded plastic that withstands years of use and abuse. They come in more or less the same sizes as aquariums, from 20 gallons to 100 gallons (76 to 380 liters), sometimes larger. However, they are easier to maintain, lighter, and less likely to break than aquariums. Because the cages have five sides made of heavy material (only the

Although effective housing for many types of reptiles, laboratory cages are expensive.

front is glass), they are easily stacked. However, those of an unusual tapered shape—not rectangular—need a special frame to hold them.

If they had the choice and the money, a majority of keepers of small to moderately large snakes and many types of lizards would likely use glass-fronted plastic or fiberglass cages. They look so nice and are easy to keep clean. Most have cutouts on top or in the sides to add basking and full-spectrum lights. The walls also can be drilled to affix misters and other devices. Unfortunately, they tend to run about five to ten times the cost of a glass aquarium of similar size.

Display Cages

Display cages usually are made of heavy particle board, typically with a waterproof veneer, and have two or three large units built in. Each unit has sliding glass doors at the front. Display cages, usually used for snakes and some lizards and turtles, are commonly 3 feet wide and 6 feet

Backup Equipment

If you get a laboratory cage, be sure to buy and safely store an extra glass front. The edge of the glass is often chipped, which can lead to cracks. Finding usable glass locally may be impossible or very expensive. Consider purchasing an extra pair of rails as well. The rails often accumulate bedding material that makes it difficult to slide the glass and may warp or damage the rails themselves. Some cages are made so the rails can be changed if they warp. Other cages simply have a groove worked into the plastic instead of rails.

high (91 and 183 cm). A single unit may be from 2 to 3 feet (61 to 91 cm) high. They are beautiful to look at, but they are difficult to heat or to fit with basking lights because of their tight, unified construction, which doesn't allow placing of lights or heaters at the top and bottom of the cages. Beware of units that have light sockets installed inside the cage—this will lead to severe burns on any snake or lizard unfortunate enough to be housed in that cage. Display cages are great for nonbaskers such as corn snakes, kingsnakes, and some boas and pythons.

Mesh Cages

The past decade has seen the development of vertical cages made completely of fine mesh supported by PVC plastic tubes. The mesh may be of fiberglass, nylon, or plastic. To assemble, you just put the frame together, pull the mesh over the frame, and zip or Velcro it shut. The mesh is strong enough to survive a basking light placed a foot (0.3 m) or more from the cage. The cages can even be fitted to hang from a tree branch outdoors.

The mesh cages were designed mostly for keeping chameleons (*Chamaeleo* spp. and allies) and geckos, which like tall cages with lots of climbing branches and extensive ventilation. It's easy to mist the mesh cage or affix an automatic misting or water dripper unit over it; some cages even come with a plastic base to hold excess water from the mister. Most come in black or white material and provide fairly good visibility of the lizard within. Mesh cages are relatively inexpensive. Many keepers of chameleons have several, some indoors and others outdoors.

Mesh cages work well for small lizards such as chameleons.

These cages are not meant to hold amphibians (which will dehydrate quickly) and aren't trustworthy with even a moderately large snake (which can force open most zippers and Velcro fastenings). You can try them for smaller kingsnakes and such that might like to go outdoors for some sun and air on occasion. Large lizards such as green iguanas and monitors will rip the mesh to shreds in seconds. They also need hotter basking lights than these cages can withstand. As you may expect, anoles (*Anolis* spp.) and similar small climbing lizards are right at home in these cages.

Premade Iguana Cages

Several years ago, manufacturers of bird cages started offering modified models that accommodate small to medium green iguanas and other larger lizards that like tall cages with lots of ventilation. These are gigantic bird cages with heavy steel wire on all sides, often with a mesh spacing of about 1 to 1½ inches (2.5 to 3.7 cm). The screen may be square mesh or mostly horizontal wires with some vertical support wires; both allow a lizard to climb easily. In many cases, these cages are outfitted with one or two basking shelves of metal or plastic. Some have a heavy base that slides out for easy cleaning, much as the base of a bird cage does. Most are on wheels so they can be easily moved or taken outside on a nice day.

Other than being relatively expensive (prices are coming down slowly), there is little to fault in premade iguana cages. Assuming they are well made, have no projecting wires, and have a top heavy enough to support lights (a few models even have a false ceiling between the lights and the iguana's living space, making them very safe), they are a good investment if you plan to keep one or two iguanas or similar herps. Their one problem is size—most are no more than 3 or 4 feet (91 or 122 cm) long and 5 feet (152 cm) high, which really is too small for a fully grown male green iguana. However, these cages are better than most homemade cages and probably more durable; taking your iguana out for a walk each day may compensate for any crowding. Larger models certainly will be widely available in the future.

Do-It-Yourself

Although this book does not contain detailed plans for making your own vivarium, it doesn't hurt to talk about what a homemade cage should include. There is very little reason to try to build your own small cage for indoor use today. However, many keepers still like to try to modify into a herp cage an old piece of furniture such as a wooden TV cabinet or a chest of drawers, especially for use with snakes and lizards. More keepers try to build their own outdoor cages for iguanas, monitors, and similar large species. We'll talk about building some simple outdoor cages in a later chapter.

Keepers often make their own outdoor cages. Like many of these cages, this one has been built to hang from a tree.

Remember that most herps are escape artists. They will get through small cracks and holes or rush between your legs if you have a walk-in cage. Some may try to dig out of a cage placed on the lawn. The easiest escape points are the corners (herps are drawn to corners) and places where panels and doors come together. You may have to use metal flashing in such areas to reinforce the structure and make it more secure.

In any cage, the door must be easily closable yet large enough to allow you to reach all corners of the cage for cleaning and catching the herp. Small doors lead to neglect and dirty cages. It just becomes too hard to get into those corners and clean them regularly. In some regions, you may be required by law to have a lock on any cage holding a

This vivarium has a locking mechanism to prevent escapes. Use a secure locking mechanism for any vivarium holding venomous animals.

snake over 10 or 12 feet (3 to 3.7 meters) long, a venomous snake, or even a large iguana or monitor (considered dangerous animals in some regions). Hardware stores sell locks made for sliding glass doors that will work with many glass-fronted cages.

This cage has been placed in a good location in the house: it is in a quiet area and near electrical outlets. Never put a cage next to a window or an air conditioner.

Positioning Cages

Use common sense when placing any cage. Never put a cage in front of a window. Direct sunlight can make a glass cage an inferno, and drafts can make a mesh cage a wind tunnel. Avoid areas that are heavily trafficked, as many herps never really adapt to lots of noise and commotion. However, if you put the cage in a closet or unused room of the house, you may find it too easy to neglect regular maintenance or even feeding—out of sight, out of mind. A quiet corner away from the TV works well. Be sure that you have enough outlets near the cage to handle the lights, heaters, misters, timers, and other devices you probably will be adding.

House your animals in a raised vivarium such as this one. Herps become nervous if a keeper's hand reaches into their habitat from above.

Air conditioners play havoc with reptiles, creating drafts and cold spots that can lead to respiratory diseases. However, many amphibians do best at low air temperatures and prefer a heavily air-conditioned area below 70°F (21°C) all year. Find out which applies to your herp.

Place all your herp cages in a single room dedicated just to them (the herp room), if possible. This will make it easier to keep the air temperature at the right level all year, reducing your use of heaters with each cage and thus electrical costs. It also will be easier to do all your herp chores at one time and to make sure the door to the room is locked to discourage thefts and accidental intruders.

Cage Height

Most herps prefer that a hand come into their cage at their eye level, not from above, so try to place the cage at waist level or nearly so. A cage on the floor will lead to a nervous herp, and one above your shoulders will be difficult to get into.

A vivarium is designed as much to keep intruders out as to keep an animal in. Keep this in mind if you have cats or dogs, which seem to be especially attracted to the scurrying movements of small lizards and the plodding of turtles. If you let your warm-blooded pets into the herp area, all vivaria must be secure enough to prevent accidents. Better yet, keep other pets away from your herps, even if you have to install a pet gate across the doorway to the herp area.

CHAPTER 2

SUBSTRATES

Once you have decided on the best type of cage for your herp, you have to decide what type of litter to place on the bottom. You can keep substrates simple or make them very elaborate; they can be inexpensive or expensive. Some substrates work better than others for certain herps. A frog, for instance, requires a moist substrate, whereas a desert-dwelling lizard requires sand. Your choice of substrate material will obviously depend to a great extent on what type of animal you are keeping. As we will see, some substrates work poorly with reptiles and amphibians and are more appropriate for mice or birds. Never underestimate the importance of the proper substrate for the health of your pet.

There are many possible cage substrates. Shown here are gravel, sand, soil, and pebble substrates.

Newspaper

Although many hobbyists don't like to admit it, the easiest and probably most commonly used reptile substrate is still newspaper. This paper stock, which usually is made from pulp of low-quality pine or related trees, can be thought of as pine shavings that have been soaked and compressed to the ultimate degree. Some hobbyists like to use old newspapers as the lining for their simple snake cages, and certainly corn snakes, kingsnakes, boas, and pythons seldom object to just having a few sheets of yesterday's paper in the bottom of their cages. Old newspaper is inexpensive—possibly even free—and easy to replace daily. It absorbs water and waste fairly well and is easy to dispose of after use.

Old newspapers are covered with printer's ink, which uses alcohol of various types as a solvent. Here we face an interesting problem. Some hobbyists believe that ink actually reduces the growth of bacteria and increases the general health of the cage. Others believe that ink is toxic and should never be in contact with a reptile. (Today's soy-based inks, which are becoming more common, seem to be less toxic than older metallic pigment-based inks.) Both sides cannot be right, but it must be mentioned that old newspapers, complete with ink, were used and still are used in cages (during quarantine or for ill herps) at zoos and vet offices, and they were widely used for at least fifty years before the fear of ink began. Make your own choice, but I've never seen any evidence that inks are harmful to herps.

You can avoid the problem entirely by using unprinted newspaper stock. Many small newspapers, including your local shopper or town news, will sell you an end roll of newsprint. This is the residue of a roll of newspaper stock

A keeper lines the bottom of a vivarium with newspaper. Inexpensive and easy to change, newspaper is often used as substrate in sterile setups.

that was too short to efficiently print. An end roll may be 2 feet (61 cm) wide or more and contain 10 to 50 feet (3 to 15 meters) of paper, all pristine and uncontaminated with ink. End rolls are relatively inexpensive, the yellowish-white newspaper stock looks good, and you should be able to find them locally. Be sure to get only a coarse, uncoated newspaper stock (which will absorb liquids), not the shiny white clay-coated stock used for printing in color—shiny stock does not absorb well.

Carpet

Some hobbyists think that newspaper looks bad on the bottom of a cage and detracts from their herps. They prefer more sophisticated bedding materials. Perhaps the most commonly seen replacement in the cages of large snakes and lizards is carpeting. Sections of carpet can be purchased in various shades of green or tan that look quite natural with a boa or a python. Indoor-outdoor carpeting is soft to the touch and nonabrasive; it usually comes with a heavy, waterproof liner that keeps water and wastes from leaking onto the bottom of the cage. The carpet part gets dirty quickly, but waste can be cleaned off when it dries, and the entire carpet can be taken out and washed (in a washer or hosed off, depending on size and circumstances) before being sun dried. A good grade of indoor-outdoor carpeting should last several months if kept clean.

If you buy two or three similar size pieces of carpeting, you can easily replace the dirty one with a clean one while the first is being washed and dried. Carpeting rolls up for easy storage, so the spares won't take much space in your herp room or closet.

You also can use indoor-outdoor carpeting as a base under mosses and litter in a more natural-looking vivarium. The problem here is that the carpet stays wet most of the time and eventually will rot or grow bacteria. Your cage should be able to withstand some wet substrate, so using carpeting under other bedding is a waste of time. One exception may be if you use sand in a desert vivarium, which will allow you to more easily prevent spreading and loss of the bedding material.

Astroturf

Astroturf, a type of carpet with a very open backing and erect, hard plastic, grasslike "leaves," once was widely recommended for cages. However, this material is much too hard for the belly of a snake and can actually abrade the scales. In addition, water and waste pass through the carpet and end up on the floor of the cage under the carpet, where they help form a not-so-lovely bacterial culture. Avoid Astroturf and similar products. The same applies to plastic runner materials, which are cheap but not absorbent and will eventually cause your cage to either rot if made of wood or become very unsanitary.

Moss

If you keep amphibians or some types of small ground-dwelling lizards (especially skinks), you probably will want some mosses in your vivarium. Moss looks natural and appropriate with salamanders and frogs, and it helps maintain a humid environment and soft substrate. Collecting your own moss is possible in many areas that have high humidity, but never collect from parks or preserves. Mosses grow slowly and may take years to cover just a few feet of ground; they help hold the soil together until higher plants can live in the soil, preventing erosion. Most mosses also do poorly in the low light levels and constant temperatures of the vivarium, so they have to be replaced on a regular basis to stay looking good.

Living sphagnum moss, which holds a lot of moisture, is a popular substrate for moist vivaria.

Sphagnum moss (genus *Sphagnum*), a special type of moss that has cells that hold a tremendous amount of water, often is sold as living moss for the vivarium. It is offered in the form of flat sheets or small bales with a bit of adhering soil and often a few contaminating higher plants. Living sphagnum can be quite expensive, but it looks really great in a moist vivarium, lasts, and makes many animals feel at home. Additionally, it releases chemicals that help maintain a slightly acid pH in the substrate and may reduce bacterial growth. Unless your backyard is covered with mosses, spend a few dollars to buy some living sphagnum.

Sand

Sand is a natural choice for desert lizards and snakes, including burrowing boas such as Kenyan sand boas (*Eryx colubrinus*). Use a good grade of clean white sand such as that sold for use in children's sandboxes (play sand). This type of sand is uniform in grain size, the grains are relatively rounded, and the sand has been sanitized before sale. Never use sand meant for construction purposes—it has large sharp grains and often is contaminated with other materials and chemicals. Stick with sandbox sand.

Sand has problems you should be aware of. First, it is hard to keep at a uniform moisture level, although it does absorb waste matter well. It dries up too fast for some types of burrowing lizards unless you add water to the corners of the cage on a regular basis to provide moist areas. Sand also cools down rapidly after the basking light is turned off, and you may get unwanted temperature drops at night. (This may not be a problem for most desert reptiles. They are adapted to tolerate or even need cool nighttime temperatures.) Sand also spreads—it is almost impossible to keep inside a vivarium that is not a closed box, such as an aquarium. You will find it very difficult to use sand in a vivarium with sliding front glass panels, even if you add an extra-high lip behind the panels.

Some hobbyists also have a perpetual fear that their lizards or snakes will eat some sand grains with their food and this will result in an intestinal impaction. This has happened on occasion, so there is some basis for this fear. However, you must remember that reptiles living in sandy

deserts are probably constantly taking in sand with their prey. If impactions occur in the vivarium, they possibly are due to captivity-induced weaknesses in the herp. The weakness prevents the herp from correctly processing the food and the sand it takes in. A common feeding practice also increases the chances of impaction: feeding moist foods. To make calcium–vitamin D_3 supplement powder stick to a mouse, salad, or some mealworms, many keepers lightly mist or dip the food in water and then add the powder. However, in addition to helping the powder stick to the food, the moisture allows many sand grains to stick to the food. If you must feed moistened foods, place them on a wide feeding plate or at least a paper towel, or feed the herp in a separate cage with a sand-free bottom.

Recently, calcium carbonate in a sandlike form has been sold under various brand names for use in the desert vivarium. Yes, reptiles can eat this calcium "sand" without too many problems, but it is far from natural. Real sand is silicon dioxide, not calcium carbonate, and even sand derived in part from decomposed shells contains a different type of calcium carbonate (aragonite versus calcite). Calcium carbonate absorbs water and breaks down into a slush under some circumstances. It is not a reliable source of calcium for your herps and perhaps is not even metabolized into a useful form of calcium in the body. Is calcium sand harmful? Probably not. Is it necessary? Definitely not. However, it comes in a variety of colors (including glow-in-the-dark!), some of which really provide a great accent for your bearded dragon (genus *Pogona*). If you want to use it, think of it as a design feature, and use it sparingly to bring out contrasts in the vivarium decor; don't think of it as a food supplement.

Rocks

Gravel often is used as a base under wood litters of various types (to reduce water buildup in the litter). Gravel is important if you must use a filter in a water body, such as in a turtle cage. However, gravel makes a poor bedding material by itself. It is completely nonabsorbent, is usually abrasive (no matter how rounded the particles seem), and sometimes is eaten by a herp (by accident or on purpose) and can lead to intestinal impactions. Gravel works well in an aquarium, but it seldom is useful in a vivarium. Small amounts of colored aquarium gravel with an inert coating can be used as decoration, but it is best to put the gravel in an area not often frequented by your pet.

Larger rocks, such as pieces of slate or flat rocks from stream beds, can be used for accent pieces and as basking spots. Rocks absorb a lot of heat, and many herps prefer to bask on rocks placed under a basking light. Of course, rocks also lose their heat quickly when the light is turned off.

If you use rocks as decorations and plan to stack them, remember that if they tumble they can easily crush a herp.

Although gravel works well as a filter in a wet setup, it can be abrasive.

Many herps use rock slabs such as these for basking and for hiding.

Use silicone cement to hold rocks safely in position. Carefully cemented rocks make interesting and useful retreats for many herps.

Alternative Beddings

You will find a wide range of nontraditional bedding materials being sold in pet supply shops. Few of these have ever become popular, as they really are not an improvement over standard bedding materials and are much more expensive.

Ground walnut shells provide an interesting brown, textured material that some hobbyists like to use in small patches in a lizard vivarium. The material packs well into a nearly solid block when wet so you can control its spread and restrict it to small areas of the cage. It is probably harmless if eaten (although I've heard of impactions from this material, as from almost any other). It is said to be dustless, but this seldom proves to be the case. It is several times more expensive than sand—even the best quality sand—and is best used in small amounts as a design element.

Cat Litter

Most cat litters are based on a type of absorbent clay, and they simply are not safe to use in a vivarium. They may absorb lots of water, but they also are dusty, cannot be digested, and could kill your lizard or snake. Avoid clay cat litters of any type.

Coconut husks have entered the market recently under several names. These are the chopped, processed hairs of the husk around the actual coconut (some beddings based on processed coconut shells also are sold). This is the material that is used to make those hairy welcome mats you see at back-door entrances. It absorbs a good bit of water and might have a place in an amphibian vivarium, but its value and problems are really unexplored. Coconut fiber often is sold in the form of bricks that are soaked to decompress the material, much like some forms of sphagnum.

Reprocessed paper is a fairly popular bedding material sold under several brand names, but it usually is in the form of irregular grayish bits that are very absorbent. This material tends to be extremely dusty, almost like cat litter, and eventually breaks down into a grayish sludge that is unsightly and probably not safe. When kept dry, however, it proves to be a satisfactory substrate that absorbs wastes well and has a fairly long and useful life. Unfortunately, it has a strange odor that some people cannot tolerate. Although you might think that paper would be cheap, most brands are actually quite expensive. If you use reprocessed paper litter in a bearded dragon vivarium, change it frequently before it decomposes.

The same general advice about use of reprocessed paper would apply to bedding made from processed corn cobs. This granular material is very dusty and so light that it moves too much to use in a vivarium with an active lizard or snake. Watch out for intestinal impactions, as it is likely to get on any food and in the water bowl as well.

Mulch

Many hobbyists like to use various types of hardwood mulch (cypress mulch is one of the most popular) as the bedding for their vivaria. Mulch, if of a uniform size and quality, looks good and natural and can absorb a lot of water and waste before having to be changed. It smells natural, and it seldom is eaten by herps. (There have been impactions from eating mulch, but they are not common.) You often can find a suitable mulch at a local garden supply store, but be careful to get one that is uniform in size and doesn't contain large chunks or partial branches that have to be removed to make spreading and cleaning easier. Some hobbyists like a fine mulch; others prefer chips. Chips usually do better in large cages with large lizards and snakes, although they can abrade the belly of a big snake. There always is a danger that a layer of mulch will become too moist for many snakes (such as corn snakes and kingsnakes) and could lead to bacterial infections of the belly scutes. Check the moisture in the mulch regularly, sniff it to detect the sour smell of bacterial growth, and replace it as soon as you believe it is overstaying its welcome in the vivarium.

Special mulch mixes are widely sold in pet supply shops. These are an excellent choice because they are uniform in size and quality. Some mixes are sold as orchid bark, which may contain vermiculite or perlite (both processed minerals that can absorb a great amount of water relative to their weight) and even fertilizers. Never use any mix that contains or might contain fertilizer—it will kill your herps. Some keepers fear perlite as well, worrying that small lizards may

Cypress mulch works well as a substrate in a naturalistic cage.

be attracted to it, may swallow it, and then may die of impactions. Vermiculite, by contrast, seems to be fairly safe in the vivarium in small quantities, although it is most often used in incubators because it can hold so much water relative to its weight.

Mulch Contaminants

Mulch from your local garden center is far from sterile. It often contains mites, various small insects, and seeds, all of which could be a nuisance or even danger in the vivarium. Before adding commercial mulch to the vivarium, spread it out in a thin layer in a dry, very sunny spot for a few days to let the sun get rid of most contaminants. Some people have microwaved mulch or baked it in the oven, both processes that have dangerous possible side effects, including fires and the release of toxic gases. They are not recommended.

Mulch often is dyed red or other colors to increase contrast in the flower bed, but you don't want this in your vivarium. The dyes wash out eventually, and it is not certain that they are safe for reptiles and amphibians. Buy mulch without dyes.

Horticultural mulch often contains large amounts of soil, so it may be necessary to wash it first to remove the soil and then dry it to remove other contaminants. Pet supply shop mulch mixtures may be more expensive than horticultural mulch, but they generally have fewer contaminants and may have already been heat-treated to kill pests.

Pine and Aspen

For most snake, lizard, and turtle vivaria, a good grade of clean, uniform pine or aspen shavings is the most efficient and economical bedding material. Both materials are very clean as a rule (with pine being a bit dustier at the bottom of the bag), look quite natural after a day or two under a herp, absorb water and waste well, don't smell, seldom are eaten (so they will not cause impactions), and are cheap enough to replace regularly. Aspen is a bit more expensive than pine but contains none of the oils that sometimes are found in pine shavings. Some keepers avoid pine because of the oils, but this probably is an unfounded fear, especially consider-

Aspen and pine shavings are clean, inexpensive, and attractive substrate options.

ing most pine used as bedding is heat-treated to remove much of the oils. Aspen is virtually dust free and more uniform than pine. Both bedding materials are widely available, often in economy-size bags that store well. Compressed pine and aspen chips also are available, but they are too expensive at the moment to use in average vivaria.

Use a base of about 1 to 2 inches (2.5 to 5 cm) of shavings in a typical cage, perhaps a bit more in the corners where reptiles tend to defecate more. The shavings under a water bowl will get wet, but it is easy to remove the wet material and spread drier shavings into place each day. Shavings are easy to handle even when dirty and wet, unlike some other bedding materials that decompose into sludge.

Cedar

In the confines of a vivarium, it probably is not safe to use cedar shavings as a bedding material. The volatile oils in cedar that give it its distinctive smell are thought by some keepers and vets to cause kidney and respiratory problems in herps and also to possibly lead to tumors. There is little scientific evidence to back up these claims, but most keepers believe that lizards, snakes, and amphibians live shorter lives in vivaria with cedar. Play it safe and avoid cedar shavings.

CHAPTER 3

LANDSCAPING AND DECORATIONS

V iews differ on how to decorate a vivarium. Some keepers prefer a clean, simple look virtually devoid of any but the most essential furniture, whereas others like a naturalistic vivarium with a variety of plants, furniture, and even specialty backdrops. Keeping the decorations simple makes it easier to see your pet and to keep the vivarium clean. Many herps can become "lost" in a naturalistic vivarium, especially one that is heavily planted. Dangerous herps such as venomous snakes and nervous pythons generally are kept in simple surroundings so it is easier and safer to catch them and to clean the cages.

Some keepers prefer naturalistic vivaria such as the one shown here; others think the animals get lost in these elaborate types of setup.

Each keeper will make his or her own decision about how heavily to decorate the vivarium, but remember that if it is difficult to get into a vivarium for regular cleaning, waste is more likely to accumulate in remote corners. Living plants have special lighting and humidity needs that often conflict with the needs of the herp. Make your decision carefully, and always consider the health of your pet first. Beginning keepers are urged to start with simple vivaria and move to more naturalistic ones only after they gain experience.

Branches

Almost any vivarium for a basking snake or lizard should have at least one or two branches positioned under the basking light. Most arboreal lizards simply will not bask comfortably on the floor of the vivarium, preferring to be near the top. Many snakes like to drape themselves over a branch and spend their days or nights contemplating their navels. (Yes, snakes have navels, or at least a shallow slit representing where the yolk sac or placenta was attached to the belly.) Branches also look good in a vivarium, and they often are the only decorative items that really look natural.

A variety of branch types is available at pet supply stores. Among the most common are decorative branches and standing "trees" made by sand-blasting gnarly grape vines or grape roots. These branches look great and last almost forever, are available in a variety of lengths and

Like the tenants of this vivarium, most herps will utilize branches for climbing and basking.

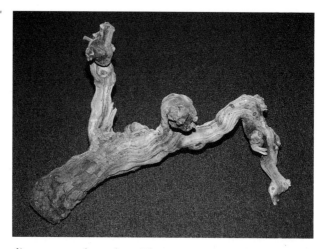

Grape vines make excellent, natural-looking vivaria decorations.

diameters, and are clean. They are expensive, but they are a good investment and can be used in almost any type of vivarium.

The meshlike woody ribs of the cholla cactus, which look best in desert surroundings, are also sold in lengths that can be used as basking and decorative branches. They have the disadvantage, however, of being so open that small herps can wedge themselves into the wood and be almost impossible to retrieve. Use cholla wood only with larger species. Another interesting branch now being sold for use in vivaria is manzanita, which has a unique gloss and is often a purplish color.

Cholla branches are commonly used in cages housing large herps.

You may choose to cut your own branches or pick them off the ground. This is fine, especially if the branches are from hardwood trees that aren't likely to give off resins and oils. Be sure that you thoroughly clean every branch before adding it to the vivarium, as a multitude of little insects (including dangerous ants) live under the bark and in the branch itself. Soak all branches in bleach for at least an hour, rinse them under running water, and then let them sit in a container of clean water for half a day. Try to peel off as much bark as possible while still allowing the branches to look natural. Never use insect sprays or soap on branches.

If you collect branches yourself, wash them with bleach before placing them in the cage.

Usually, branches are simply wedged from corner to corner of a vivarium, which makes them secure enough to take the weight of even a heavy lizard or snake. To remove a branch for cleaning with this type of setup, you have to basically take the cage apart, but you won't have to clean it very often. You also can use hooks and eyes to attach a branch horizontally across a vivarium, allowing it to sway a bit in a natural way and also to be easily removed for cleaning. To attach it, simply screw an eye into each end of the perch and a hook with a spring retainer into the adjacent wall or roof. Hardware stores carry a wide range of hook and eye sets in many sizes and styles. Purchased branches such as those used in cages for large parrots often have bolts inserted into the ends that fit into metal sockets

Artificial branches
such as these are
readily available at
most pet supply
stores and can be
manipulated to fit
many different
spaces.

affixed to the walls of the vivarium; this may be the easiest way of attaching a branch. If you try to place an erect, free-standing branch in the vivarium, you probably will have to brace it at the bottom as well as run a screw through the base into the branch. Because of the weight of basking snakes and the force that a jumping lizard can impart to a free-standing branch, only short, thick branches are safe to use in this way.

When fixing a branch into a vivarium, remember that the closer it is to the top of the cage, the more force a snake or large lizard can apply to the lid of the cage. This also means that the herp will be closer to the hot basking light and more subject to burns from metal lids. Putting in a branch that leads directly into an upper corner of the vivarium where the lid is only weakly anchored is asking for an escape attempt.

Artificial branches made from plastic, resin, or even hollow ceramics are widely sold. Some of the plastic types can be bent and used in areas where a natural branch won't fit. Ceramic branches generally look artificial and don't fit into the decor of almost any vivarium, but recently some nicer examples have been offered. Artificial branches fitted with heating strips to give basking lizards and snakes warm bellies are sold, but they usually have the same disadvantages as heat rocks (see the lighting and heating chapter) and really aren't necessary.

Bamboo

There is a long tradition of using bamboo in vivaria, especially rain forest and woodland vivaria, and it is certainly worth following. Bamboos are giant grasses with hard, very tough hollow stems broken into segments by thin partitions at nodes visible as rings on the outsides of the stems. They may be only an inch (2.5 cm) or less in diameter (when they usually are called canes) or as much as 3 to 4 inches (7.6 to 10 cm). Once harvested, bamboo lasts virtually forever in a vivarium and does not rot when subjected to water. Intact or vertically split lengths of bamboo can be drilled and fastened together with monofilament fishing line to make interesting backdrops. Intact lengths of bamboo stem can be positioned strategically in a vivarium as points of interest. Many small lizards, frogs, and snakes will take up residence in horizontally cut bamboo stems, which also accumulate water at the nodes below a cut. For some herps, such as tropical tree frogs and leaf frogs (*Agalychnis* spp.) and many day geckos (*Phelsuma* spp.), bamboo segments (wet for frogs, dry for geckos) make excellent retreats.

Some bamboos and bamboolike grasses are sold as living specimens, but they seldom survive for long and are not a good investment. Additionally, living bamboos are often too tall for vivaria. Stick with good quality bamboo stems, available from many dealers.

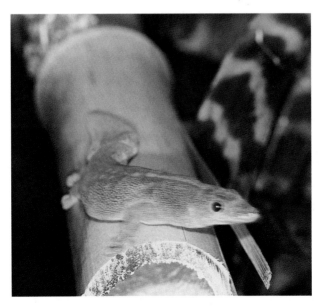

Small lizards, such as this day gecko, will use cut bamboo stems for hiding and basking.

Backdrops

One simple way to brighten up a vivarium at little cost is to use a printed backdrop. These are large sheets of heavy paper or plastic printed with colorful natural scenes that vary from rain forest habitat to sandy desert floors with cacti in the distance. Backdrops also are available in single colors, from subdued greens and blues to iridescent reds and even glow-in-the-dark colors. Originally made for use with aquariums, where they were placed behind the back glass to help hide air lines and electrical cords, most printed backdrops are still made in sizes and proportions to fit the walls of standard-size aquariums. This is where they work best.

A backdrop allows you to easily darken the back and sides of a glass or mesh vivarium, which increases the feeling of security for your pet and allows you to hide that ugly blank wall behind the vivarium. It also can be used inside a vivarium cage with opaque sides. However, it is more likely to be torn or dirtied by the movements of the herp and certainly will become wavy from moisture in the vivarium. Printed backdrops usually are just taped to the sides of the vivarium using transparent tape. If you place one inside the cage, it is best to use double-sided tape along every edge of the backdrop to reduce damage and keep herps from going behind it.

Pick your backdrop carefully. Using the wrong type (a beach scene for a rain forest reptile, for instance) will detract

Purchased backdrops, such as this desert landscape print, can enhance the aesthetics of a naturalistic vivarium.

Some keepers may opt for a three-dimensional backdrop; this one is constructed of styrofoam.

from the reptile or amphibian. The purpose of the backdrop is not only to hide uninteresting walls in the vivarium but also to accent the beauty and uniqueness of your pet.

If a printed backdrop is not for you, you can make more elaborate three-dimensional backdrops by cutting a sheet of Masonite or a similar strong, thin material (foam-core art board is thicker but very stable) to fit the vivarium on the back or sides. Paint the board with an animal-safe spray paint so it resembles the substrate or habitat you want to mimic. Depending on the habitat, shades of green or tan work well. Then stick bits of cork bark (available in many sizes and textures from pet shops), moss, real and artificial leaves, bits of vines, and similar decorative items to the board. Silicone cement and hot glue both work well to adhere decorative elements to the board. Be sure that any heavy items (such as stones near the bottom) are securely anchored, preferably tied in place with fine wire run through holes in the board. You can even attach small flowerpots to the backdrop (use wire or hot glue) to hold interesting plants well above the bottom of the vivarium. The object of the exercise is to help give the vivarium the impression of greater size and complexity than reality, while also offering your pet a few more perches or places to explore.

To position this complex backdrop inside a glass vivarium, glue the backdrop to the glass with dabs of silicone cement. Place the dabs of cement so they can be reached and cut through to remove the backdrop if necessary. In wooden or fiberglass vivaria, screw or bolt the backdrop into place. Any hole through the vivarium should be covered with a wide washer just in case tiny lizards or snakes consider escaping. Glue molding strips across the bottom, top, and sides to make sure the herp cannot get under the backdrop. Make sure that no flammable items on the backdrop come too close to the basking light or heater. If you are using an aquarium for the vivarium, you can also hang the backdrop outside the cage with strong wire hooks, making sure the backdrop does not interfere with the security of the aquarium lid.

Hide Boxes

Almost every herp needs a cozy little retreat to escape the pressures of captivity and get a good night or day of sleep. You can find a variety of hide boxes in any pet supply shop or make your own from discarded cereal boxes or cardboard tubes from paper towel rolls. What you use depends on whether you care how natural your vivarium appears. Again, as long as a hide box is dark and cozy (most herps like to feel the sides of the box when they nap), the herp won't care what it looks like.

Pieces of naturally curved cork bark (taken in strips from Spanish cork oaks and sold with virtually no treatment or enhancement) are widely available and are a great natural-

An inventive keeper fashioned a coconut husk into a hide box.

Small herps will make use of hide boxes fashioned from paper towel and toilet paper tubes.

looking type of retreat that can look good in almost any terrain. Cork bark, large or small strips of natural bark harvested from cork oak trees, is hard to clean, but it also is fairly inert and doesn't need much attention. Good also are curved pieces of natural wood or bark (usually Pacific Northwest conifers) cut to appropriate lengths. These retreats are available in an array of widths and heights and can be found in a size to accommodate anything from a small anole to a large python. Weight may be a consideration with the largest pieces, however.

Recently, some manufacturers have begun producing hide boxes made of foam and resin that resemble natural rocks of various types. These are just as good as any other hide box and certainly look more natural than that old cereal box. Some of these artificial rocks even are hinged or cut to allow them to be opened to reveal the napping herp—and retrieve a specimen that is reluctant to come out for examination. The prices of these pieces can be high.

Feeding Dishes

Every herp needs a dish for its food and a dish for its water. If you want something cheap, you can use the discarded plastic trays from TV dinner entrées. They work well, often are inconspicuously black, and can be thrown away after a few days of use. Most keepers, however, prefer fancier dishes for their charges, and manufacturers have been more than willing to comply with consumer wishes. Dishes are avail-

Food and water bowls come in many different styles, shapes, and sizes.

able in a variety of sizes and depths and can be found in ceramic and resin compositions that look like natural rocks. They are nonporous and won't leak; they are also tough and hard to break. Their broad base and low profile make them hard to turn over. Spend the money and get several good dishes, at least two sets, so you can put in a clean dish while the other is being washed.

If you want the ultimate dishes, you might be able to find some that are heated and some that actually vibrate to make dead food items appear alive to a lizard or snake. These are more novelties that useful items, however. Instead of using a vibrating dish to fool your leopard gecko (*Eublepharis macularius*) into taking dried crickets, put the effort into providing a good, varied, living insect diet.

TV-dinner trays make inexpensive and disposable food bowls.

Soaking Tubs

Many herps like to soak. One common problem is that your snake or lizard constantly overturns its water dish while trying to use it as a bathtub. Adding to the problem is the fact that many herps actually prefer to defecate in their water dish, leading to foul conditions and the chance of illness. One solution is to give your herp a separate soaking tub.

The tub will vary greatly depending on the herp being served. A frog or salamander can use a container just a bit larger and deeper than the water dish and be quite comfortable. A large Burmese python (*Python molurus bivittatus*), which can reach a length of more than 12 feet (3.6 meters)

A turtle soaks in a large plastic tub. Many reptiles and amphibians require a soaking tub.

and may spend much of its time in the soaking tub, needs something quite different. The soaking tub should be at least one and a half times the length of the lizard's or turtle's body and about the same width. It should be the coiled diameter of a larger snake and also about the same width. This gives the herp plenty of room to move around and get comfortable without forcing too much water over the edge of the tub. Remember that heavy herps will displace more water than lighter ones, so they will need proportionately less water in the tub.

As a rule, if you offer a soaking tub, remove the water dish during the day when the herp is most likely to soak. Replace it in the morning and evening when the herp begins to bask and become active. Many larger herps may not need a smaller water bowl if given a soaking tub for just four to eight hours a day. Never leave any soaking tub in the vivarium more than one to two days without cleaning it—it is sure to be fouled with feces.

Many herps will use a large water bowl as a soaking tub, but even better are the stainless steel dishes used to feed and water dogs. These are virtually indestructible, will withstand sanitizing with bleach and boiling water for years, and won't react to the feces or develop stains. Larger snakes and lizards often can use small hard rubber or plastic stock tubs or buckets of 10 to 20 gallons (38 to 76 liters) capacity. You should have no problem finding a sturdy soaking tub to suit your herp.

Plants

As a rule, living plants are a pain in a vivarium. However, many hobbyists consider it a worthy challenge to provide living plants in their vivaria. Others believe the focus should be on keeping herps rather than plants. You can keep quite a few plants in almost any vivarium, but eventually most will die or turn brown and ugly. Plants seldom need the same type and intensity of light as do herps, and they don't do well overall in hot, humid vivaria. The only plants that will truly thrive in most humid vivaria are pothos (*Scindapsus*) and philodendrons.

This tropical vivarium features lush vegetation. When designing a naturalistic vivarium, however, try to keep the focus on the herps, not the plants.

There is no shortage, however, of plants that will live for a few weeks or even months in a vivarium. More and more pet shops are selling usable plants, and for the extreme fancier, some dealers now carry a variety of bromeliads and even orchids that will survive—for a while. In desert vivaria, cacti often are used along with aloes and other succulents, but few can stand being abused by a lizard or snake. Spiny forms are not used because they are thought to be harmful to herps (which somehow manage to negotiate extremely spiny plants in nature without being impaled!).

Herps are not really aware of whether there are living plants in their vivarium. They don't see the world that way, so living plants are more to satisfy the needs of the keeper than those of the herp.

Popular Plants

Although few plants actually do well in vivaria, some are hardier and more attractive than others and have become quite popular with keepers. Everyone who has attempted to maintain planted vivaria probably has had somewhat different results with the same species of plants. This may be due to weaknesses or strengths in a particular group of plants purchased locally, the age of the plants when purchased, the exact variety or cultivar (many plants are available in a multitude of sizes and leaf color and shape), and whether the keeper has a green thumb.

The following plants are widely available and often can be kept successfully. Try some (few are expensive), and see what works best for you.

Begonias (*Begonia* species)

If you want a cheap way of adding colorful plants to your vivarium, consider a pot or two of begonias. Although they seldom will set flowers again, these common and inexpensive plants have sturdy leaves that will live for weeks or months in a woodland terrarium with moderate humidity levels. Many species and varieties are available, but all prefer the brightest light they can get. Consider them expendable plants for interesting accents.

Although begonias are inexpensive and add color and vibrancy to your aquarium, their flowers do not live long.

Bird's-Nest Ferns (*Asplenium* species)

As a rule, ferns are too fragile to survive for long in the average vivarium (although some tropical varieties are used as background plantings in large rain forest vivaria). One major exception to this is the bird's-nest ferns (such as *Asplenium nidus*), which have wide, pointed leaves that tear easily but continue growing. The many large leaves come up tightly from a single base that can be grown in a pot of sphagnum attached to a strong branch. They may accumulate water in their base and serve as retreats for tree frogs and geckos. Give them a humid pot and moist atmosphere with moderate lighting for greatest chance of success. They generally do not like temperatures much above 85°F (29.5°C). Large specimens may be quite expensive to purchase.

Unlike most ferns, bird's-nest ferns flourish in vivaria.

Bromeliads

Widely called air plants, thousands of species of bromeliads live in the Americas, ranging from gray, viny Spanish moss (*Tillandsia usneoides*) in the southern United States to brightly colored, broad-leaved species with 6-foot (1.8-meter) flower heads in South America. Most species are too large for use in typical vivaria, but some of the smaller species of *Guzmania, Vriesea,* and *Neoregelia* have bright green leaves and red or yellow flowers and will continue to grow even when just tied or glued to a branch or set in a

Bromeliads are probably the most common plant used in vivaria.

53

As hardy as their name implies, cast iron plants do well in low light.

Hardy Chinese evergreens are attractive and useful additions to a vivarium. Small herps use them for hiding.

sphagnum basket. The larger species of *Aechmea* are among the most beautiful plants that can be added to the rain forest vivarium. In addition, they often have a water-filled recess at the bases of the leaves in which some tropical tree frogs will lay their eggs. Bromeliads usually don't need soil but instead take much of their nutrition from dust and spores in the air, using their roots mostly for anchorage, so they are not especially choosy about substrate. Few species can survive long in very wet conditions, however, rotting in a few months. Inexpensive bromeliads already in flower (the flowers may last for months before dropping off) are widely available and give a distinctive tropical touch to any warm, humid vivarium. They are almost essential in rain forest vivaria. Be aware that many small, decorative bromeliads sold in general nurseries will not survive more than a few weeks before falling apart. Flowering bromeliads may well be dead when purchased (many die after flowering) and will no longer grow, but they can last months or even a year before they start to decompose in the vivarium. Don't spend a great amount of money on a beautiful bromeliad until you have experience in the group and understand their care requirements.

Cast Iron Plants (*Aspidistra* species)

These plants, with their wide, tough leaves, have been used in poorly lit homes for more than a century and may do well in a relatively dry woodland terrarium. The bright green leaves are thin but not especially fragile and will take some abuse. Provide a rich potting soil that is dry, never wet, and keep the pot in a bright corner but not near the heat lamp. Low-growing varieties can be used in vivaria of only 20 to 50 gallons (76 to 190 liters) without growing out of control.

Chinese Evergreens (*Aglaonema* species)

These are some of the more attractive and hardy plants for the large vivarium. Chinese evergreens like warm, moist, but heavily shaded situations in an enclosure, where their wide leaves can spread out and the plants can reach full height. These are rather bushy plants that seldom are less than a foot tall and may be more than 3 feet (91 cm) tall and often are almost as wide as they are tall. They provide great cover for lizards and frogs of all types (so good you may have difficulty finding the herp again), need little care, and may even produce bright red berries on occasion. They often are stocked in larger greenhouses.

Ornamental Figs (*Ficus* species)

Everyone has seen large rubber plants (*Ficus elastica*) used as office decorations and also as accents in many zoo plantings, but obviously these small trees are too large for any but the biggest vivaria. However, the figs represent a gigantic genus with many species, and some are quite small and very adaptable to the vivarium. Small plants of weeping fig (*Ficus benjamina*) have narrow, bright green leaves that will be sought as food by iguanas and other herbivorous lizards, so you may have to place them within mesh cylinders to

Some ornamental figs do very well in vivaria.

Philodendrons are good plants for moist vivaria.

protect their leaves. They are great in large chameleon vivaria. A favorite is the creeping fig (*Ficus pumila*), which is widely sold as a pot plant at low prices and is exceptionally hardy in woodland and even moist rain forest vivaria. This is a low-growing vine fig with nearly round leaves (edible) that can be hard to kill even under the low-light conditions of most vivaria. The larger figs usually want more light than is provided by the fluorescents used in vivaria, and they may grow better and last longer if given their own spotlight. The large leaves tend to accumulate dirt and dust rapidly, but they make a fine surface for misting, allowing droplets of water to form and flow off of them naturally. The sap of many figs may cause local irritation and sometimes more dangerous allergic reactions such as erratic breathing and a drop in blood pressure, so wear gloves when tending figs if you have reason to believe you might be allergic.

Philodendrons and Pothos
(*Philodendron* and *Scindapsus* species)
Although they share wide, oval to heart-shaped green and yellowish leaves that end in a long point and a viny growth form, the several plants sold as philodendrons and pothos

Because prayer plants need warm, humid air, they do well in rain forest vivaria.

Extremely adaptable, snake plants can thrive in almost any type of vivaria.

actually belong to separate genera that are almost impossible to distinguish. Both types are kept much the same way, however, in moist soil or baskets with moist sphagnum, and will grow well and quickly at low light levels. These are one of the hardiest vivarium plants, are inexpensive, and can be easily grown, so tired plants can be replaced on a regular basis.

Philodendrons commonly are raised in flats with moist potting soil, but display plants in larger vivaria often are fixed to slabs of cork bark or sphagnum-filled wire mesh cylinders, where the aerial roots allow them to rapidly cover their substrate with bright green to yellow-green leaves on twisting stems. Philodendrons are appreciated as food by many herbivorous lizards, and the Solomon prehensile-tailed skink (*Corucia zebrata*) thrives on them.

Prayer Plants (*Maranta* species)
Popular as plants for hanging baskets, prayer plants are noted for their red and green leaves up to 4 inches (10 cm) long that slowly fold together at the midrib when the lights go off. They need moist soil and humid air as well as warm temperatures, so they are best used in rain forest and moist woodland vivaria. Their bright colors make good accents in an otherwise green vivarium.

Snake Plants (*Sansevieria* species)
Snake plants (also called tongue plants because of the shape of their leaves) are one of the hardiest vivarium plants. They are able to survive conditions ranging from humid rain forests (if you can keep their roots relatively dry) to dry desertlike habitats. They do best in rather dry, bright conditions, however, and will die if the soil in which they are planted stays wet over long periods or if they are placed in heavy shade. Commonly, they are placed in pots in large vivaria and given their own spotlights to assure proper light levels. Most species and cultivars are a foot high, with narrow tongue-shaped leaves that end in fine points and are banded in dark and light green. Some species may be over 2 feet (61 cm) high, however, and suited only for the largest vivaria. Snake plants grow rapidly under the proper conditions and

will quickly fill their pots and need to be divided. Inexpensive and easy to find, they deserve a place along with philodendrons in the vivaria of any beginning keeper.

Succulents

Many types of small succulent plants are sold that can be used in dry vivaria. Succulents, like cacti, have leaves or stems (in succulents, the stems often are modified leaves, and the leaves are not true leaves) that can hold large amounts of water and often are spiny or at least rough. Most often used are the larger, erect species of *Euphorbia*, euphorbia (also called spurges). *Euphorbia* have small green leaves that grow from spiny tufts along the edges and green bodies with three or four corners. (If you made a slice through the body from side to side and then looked at the cut area, you would see three or four distinct sharp angles, the corners of the body.) Spurges vary greatly in size, shape, and hardiness, but they are worth a try in any dry vivarium. Be aware that many species leak a blistering white sap from cuts or breaks that may cause painful local reactions in humans.

Very useful are the many species of *Gasteria* and *Haworthia*, both of which look like kitchen aloes with broad-based triangular leaves growing in a rosette from a central point. Some are spiny, others smooth, but all do well with moderately bright light and warm temperatures in dry

This euphorbia specimen, or spurge, is one type of succulent; succulents are commonly used in desert vivaria.

surroundings. They tend to be low-growing plants only 4 to 6 inches (10 to 15 cm) high and make great background plantings. As long as these succulents are not overwatered, they will do very well in the vivarium.

Artificial Plants

There are some truly realistic and tough artificial plants available, although they tend to be more expensive than living plants. They will last a long time, however, and can be removed for easy cleaning. Artificials look almost as good as living plants, and the herps don't care if they are real or fake. Always use the best quality artificials you can find, not the cheap ones from the variety store that will fade and quickly droop. Quality artificials are available from herpetological supply catalogs and advertisers in reptile magazines and over the Internet.

What do you look for in an artificial plant? First, remember that the herp will not worry too much about whether the plant is lifelike as long as it provides a comfortable retreat and is sturdy enough to withstand being walked or crawled on. For many herps, leaves are noted mostly as the place where droplets of water accumulate after a misting—a place to take a lick of water. As a hobbyist, however, you probably will want artificials that are at least fairly faithful imitations of appropriate plants for the vivarium. For instance, although you may find it impossible to grow a rubber tree (*Ficus elastica*) in your vivarium, a high-quality

Many realistic-looking artificial plants, such as the ones shown here, are now available and offer certain advantages over live plants, which rarely last long in vivaria.

imitation will serve the same purpose, look just as good (sometimes you have to actually touch the artificial to make sure it is not real), and last for years. Of course, your iguana cannot eat it, but that may be an advantage.

Try to avoid extremely brightly colored—unnaturally bright—artificials. These are jarring to the eyes and never fit into the vivarium decor. Avoid cloth plants whose leaves are made stiff from starch or another filler. The starch will dissolve after a few mistings, leaving a limp, crumpled leaf and white deposits; the filler could also be toxic. Plastic plants are overall sturdier than cloth plants and generally safer, but keep an eye out for projecting wires at the nodes where leaves and flowers are inserted.

Artificial plants designed for use in aquariums generally are limp and will not stand up correctly in a vivarium. They also are totally inappropriate types of plants for a vivarium. Elodea just looks wrong in most vivaria. In wet vivaria, aquarium artificials can be used to line the edges of pools or waterfalls.

The most useful artificial plants are simple leafy vines. They can be stretched across corners and edges of the vivarium and be allowed to drape naturally toward the bottom of the enclosure. Vines generally are sold by the foot, and good imitations can be quite expensive. They often are not very exact replicas of any real plant, but they are very efficient ways of adding a natural look to almost any nondesert vivarium at a moderate cost. They also give a small lizard or frog lots of places to exercise or hide.

Although living cacti are almost impossible to maintain for long in the desert vivarium (their light needs are just too high), there are some very nice plastic replicas for sale that will fool anyone at first glance. These replicas come in several species. One distinct advantage all of them have over living cacti is the lack of spines that could harm a lizard or a snake confined to a small vivarium enclosure. Some replicas are jarring to the eye and not very natural, so do a bit of research on the natural plants, and try to get replicas that are the right shape and have similar coloration. Flowers are not necessary on replicas and often are poorly done anyway.

CHAPTER 4

LIGHTING AND HEATING A VIVARIUM

First, you bought a decent cage for your pet, and then you found a suitable bedding material and perhaps even added some decorations. This chapter deals with the somewhat more complicated subjects of properly lighting and heating a vivarium.

Lighting

One of the more controversial subjects of vivarium care involves proper lighting. The first thing you have to remember is that herp lighting really is two subjects: light for basking heat and light for sunlight simulation and vitamin synthesis. Although the two topics overlap somewhat, they are best treated separately.

Full-Spectrum Lighting

The blood of reptiles contains many components besides blood cells, including a chemical that is the precursor to vitamin D_3. When this precursor (pre–vitamin D_3) is

These bulbs offer UV light—essential for your herp's health.

subjected to the proper wavelengths of light, it changes its chemical structure to become vitamin D_3, which is absolutely essential for proper growth. The light that works best for this synthesis is ultraviolet (UV) light, the lower end of the light spectrum, including sunlight. UV is not visible to human eyes.

Light Spectrum

Light is a complex subject, not always easy to understand. What humans see as white light is actually a blend of several distinct colors. When sunlight passes through a prism, it breaks into different colors of light that together make white light. The mnemonic ROY G BIV reminds us of the sequence of colors, from longest wavelengths to shortest: red, orange, yellow, green, blue, indigo, violet. Longer wavelengths beyond red are detected by us as heat, whereas the shortest wavelengths are known as ultraviolet (UV) light. Human eyes do not see either heat (long) or UV (short) wavelengths without artificial aid in the form of special lenses or electronic equipment.

The components of sunlight are measured as wavelengths in nanometers (nm). A nanometer is a billionth of a meter, a very small measurement that can be detected only with special gear. Visible light (violet through red) measures from 400 to 700 nm in wavelength. Heat is very long waves, over 700 nm, whereas UV is very short waves, under 400 nm. The shorter the wave, the greater its ability to penetrate matter. A sunburn is UV light penetrating and killing skin cells (and perhaps eventually causing skin cancers).

For our purposes, UV light can be broken into two groups: UVA: the longest waves (roughly 315 to 400 nm long); and UVB: the shortest waves (about 280 to 310 nm long). The UVB waves have great penetrating power in living cells and will even cause blindness in humans if people stare into a bulb emitting it.

When a reptile (and some species of amphibian) basks, its body is positioned to allow it full exposure to sunlight, including UV. In fact, reptiles need UV light to maintain their metabolism; the short waves cause many chemical reactions in the body, the one of major importance to herp keepers being the production of vitamin D from precursor chemicals in the blood. The greatest synthesis of vitamin D_3 (the form of vitamin D that is used by reptiles) occurs upon exposure to UVB, with less synthesis under UVA.

Unfortunately, most lightbulbs produce very little UV light. Incandescent bulbs, which produce light by heating up a metal filament, are designed to produce light that is almost all in the longest wavelengths, from yellow through red to heat. They produce almost no UV light of any type. Fluorescent tubes or bulbs, which produce light by stimulating electron movement in special coatings on the glass, are capable of emitting a much more varied range of wavelengths, depending in large part on the chemistry of the coatings. Because most fluorescents are designed for human eyes, they typically radiate in the blue to red part of the spectrum, producing little heat and a small amount of UV.

You've certainly seen black lights, UV-producing fluorescent bulbs that produce no visible light or a dull blue glow yet cause UV-sensitive inks on a poster or T-shirt to fluoresce brightly when bathed in the black light. These bulbs produce mostly UVA. Special plant-growth bulbs also produce a considerable amount of light at the lower end to middle of the spectrum, the region at which the pigment chlorophyll works best.

For years, reptile hobbyists used a mixture of black light tubes and plant-growth tubes to try to supply "natural" light to their basking reptiles such as green iguanas (*Iguana iguana*) and turtles. Even when used together, these were inefficient lights, but they were better than nothing. However, long exposure to black light tubes may cause temporary blindness and perhaps tumors in some reptiles, another disadvantage of the combination.

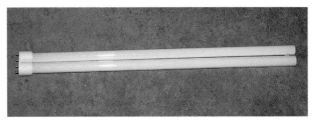

Reptiles require UVB light to synthesize vitamin D_3.

UVB Lights

Today hobbyists are lucky indeed because there now are practical, affordable full-spectrum (sunlight-equivalent) fluorescent lights that will provide their basking reptiles with not only visible light but also both UVA and a fair proportion of UVB. These tubes, which are relatively expensive but not unreasonable in cost, fit standard fluorescent fixtures and come in a variety of lengths to fit almost any cage situation. Curved and spiraled tubes that take much less space than linear tubes are now available. Like most fluorescent lights, they should be changed every six months because they weaken and their spectrum changes over time. (Mark the date of purchase on one end of the tube with a black marker to be sure you remember.)

If you are keeping heavy baskers such as iguanas or most turtles, place at least one full-spectrum light over a branch or stone that is the preferred basking spot. Try to place this light as close as possible to the animal; the UV portion becomes less efficient at greater distances. This usually means that the light and its fixture will be allowed to lie on the top of the cage, on the mesh. Most types of ordinary glass stop UV light or at least reduce its penetration, so don't bother placing full-spectrum lights over glass panes.

Most keepers use a double fixture holding two tubes, one with a full-spectrum light (which tends toward the blue end of the spectrum to our eyes) and the other with a normal daylight-white bulb. The full-spectrum light should be on for at least eight hours a day, about as long as the hot basking light.

Read the Label

Not all incandescent bulbs sold as full-spectrum bulbs really are. Read the label carefully to be sure that the bulb emits UVB as well as UVA. Most reptile-specific fluorescent tubes give off about 2 percent to 7 percent of their light in the form of UVB. Only one or two types of incandescent bulbs, actually mercury-vapor bulbs that usually require special sockets and are quite expensive, truly emit UVB light, contrary to what others might advertise. Be very careful when buying incandescent "full-spectrum" bulbs. Don't just go by the name on the package. The label must state that UVB light actually is generated.

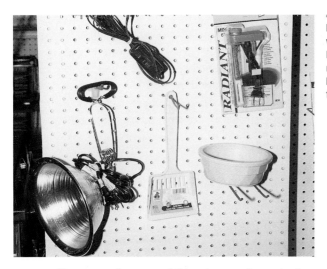

Read labels carefully when purchasing lighting. Not all commercially sold light bulbs are full spectrum lights.

Even if your reptile or amphibian is not a heavy basker, consider supplying it with full-spectrum light each day. Some frogs (such as African reed frogs, family Hyperoliidae, and some toads, genus *Bufo*) like to bask under the weak light of a single fluorescent tube for a few hours, and it never hurts to have a full-spectrum light in the vivarium of any snake, lizard, or turtle. Even those that remain hidden during the day will get some UVA and UVB to improve their vitamin D_3 synthesis. (For instance, some nocturnal geckos are thought to need very brief exposure to UVB just as the sun sets to produce vitamin D_3.) Exposure to UVA is thought to improve a reptile's color and increase its activity and appetite.

Normal Light

Everyone likes to look at their herps, and to do this, you need some normal white light or sunlight in the vivarium. A vivarium, even if kept dark, is usually in a room with windows that allow the animal to sense the passage of day and night and the seasons. This is important to maintain an animal's sense of seasons, and in some cases, to prepare it for breeding. Never keep a vivarium in a totally dark room; even a closet should be lit for at least eight hours a day.

Use a daylight fluorescent tube in a double fixture along with a full-spectrum light to provide balanced light for your

herp, especially if it is a reptile. The daylight fluorescent allows you to see the colors of your animal in an almost natural fashion and gives the herp enough light to sense day and night. Fluorescents give off relatively little heat (although the ballast or starter of the fixture may get quite hot), so it is easier to control the temperature in the vivarium.

Basking Lights

A basking light supplies heat from above for basking reptiles and the occasional basking amphibian. Many herps do not need a basking light—they are active mostly at night or under cover and seldom venture into the open during the day. Some common snakes, such as corn snakes, kingsnakes, and many boas and pythons, are largely nocturnal and will do quite well without a basking light, although they may use one if it is provided. They get enough heat for an active life from the soil and tree branches.

The traditional and still very useful basking light is an ordinary tungsten incandescent bulb of 20 to 150 watts fitted with a conical aluminum hood to concentrate the light and heat on a preferred basking spot, such as a branch or a rock. Incandescent lights are very hot, and their hoods can easily burn your hands. Take every precaution with the basking light. It must be placed outside the vivarium and far enough away that the reptile cannot burn itself on the lamp, hood, or hot wires under the light. Use a clamp to hold the light several inches (centimeters) above the top of the vivarium lid to reduce the risk of burns.

An iguana basks under an aluminum hood heat lamp.

Remember that basking lights are used for their heat, not their light. It is inefficient to waste electricity producing unwanted light, so manufacturers have produced "dark lights" strictly to produce heat rather than light. These usually are ceramic globes or disks that are coated to allow only heat to be emitted (they are often called heat emitters). Heat emitters also can be used to help heat a vivarium at night without disturbing the daily cycle of a reptile. Although they are very expensive compared with an ordinary lightbulb, heat emitters are efficient and have very long lives.

Any basking light that outputs more than 75 watts should be mounted in a ceramic socket rather than the usual metal and plastic screw-in socket. Metal sockets typically are lined with cardboard and have flimsy plastic on-off switches. They will melt or burn when used with a very hot light. Ceramic sockets are expensive but well worth the cost for their safety factor, plus they last a long time without having to be replaced or repaired.

Hoods

Some manufacturers have developed lighting hoods that fit on top of aquarium-based vivaria and even on larger vivaria. The hoods usually house several bulbs of mixed types. There may be fixtures for two fluorescent tubes and one or two incandescent bulbs for basking. Some combination light hoods may house up to six bulbs. These fixtures make it easier to watch your electrical cords, but unless each bulb is on a separate cord and switch, you may not be able to use timers or control the lighting as much as you wish.

Combination Lights

Although almost all incandescent lamps that say they produce full-spectrum lighting are exaggerating (at best), there is one type of incandescent bulb (technically a mercury-vapor lamp) available that produces both UVB and heat. This bulb, which looks like a regular lightbulb or a small spotlight, screws into a normal light socket (although ceramic is safer). It produces a hot, visible light, as well as about 2 percent of its spectrum as UVB, with some UVA as well. Since it is an incandescent, the light is more concentrated than that from a fluorescent tube and travels farther, so you still get good light even when the bulb is placed safely above the vivarium. Currently, the cost of these "solar glow" lights is very high, and some keepers have had problems with bulbs burning out quickly. However, these are highly efficient lights that combine true full-spectrum light with usable basking heat.

Photoperiod

Like most other animals, reptiles and amphibians are aware internally of the passing of days by keeping track of how long the sun (or moon) appears above the horizon each day. Many aspects of metabolism and hormone production, especially those related to reproduction, are dependent on day length, although in tropical herps there may be more reliance on keeping track of wet and dry seasons. Herps that are constantly kept in the dark, except for exclusively nocturnal, nonbasking amphibians and very few reptiles, seldom do well, are inactive, and often do not eat. Exposure to light each day increases their activity levels and appetites.

How long should you expose your animals to light, natural or artificial? This varies, depending on the type of animal and where it originated. In the tropics, close to and on the equator, day and night are of approximately equal length. In the moderately higher latitudes, both north and south, days are longer in the summer than in the winter. There are almanacs and Internet sites with complex charts that allow you to determine the actual day and night lengths almost anywhere on earth, so you can change the day length

A timer helps regulate the vivarium's photoperiod, which is handy, especially if you have a large number of reptiles or if you are away on vacation.

to match the origin of your pet, if you wish. Most reptiles and amphibians are not that delicate about day lengths, and they rapidly adjust to days in New York as well as in New Orleans or Bogotá. Reptiles are especially adaptable, and those that are captive-bred are used to northern day lengths. Unless you are fanatical (and there is little wrong with fanatical keepers, by the way), you can supply your pet with much the same day lengths as are found naturally. For instance, just give it longer days during the summer and shorter days during the winter. You also don't have to worry too much about gradually shortening or lengthening the day to match changing seasons; even indirect sunlight through windows is strong enough to easily override your artificial lights.

As a rule, most keepers provide at least eight hours of light, both full-spectrum and basking, each day. This is sufficient for almost every species. More than eight hours of light provides little for your pet and shortens the lifetime of your lights. Many reptiles are happy with only three or four hours of basking light each day (generally split between morning and later afternoon) and will move away from the basking area to a cooler spot. Watch the way your pets behave, and change the lighting accordingly.

If you have just one vivarium with two lights, it probably is not a great chore to remember to turn them on and off each day. But what happens when you go on vacation or are ill? Using timers designed for outdoor lights makes keeping a photoperiod simple. Most timers plug into an outlet and contain receptacles for two or three light cords. You set the clockwork mechanism (now digital in some expensive timers) according to instructions, and the lights go on and off as desired. Changes for the seasons are easy to make. Some timers allow you to set two separate on-off cycles, which means that you can turn off the basking light earlier than the full-spectrum, or vice versa. Be sure to buy a heavy-duty outdoor timer, not a cheap one designed for house lights; the latter has a tendency to burn out or malfunction.

Heating

In many cases, your reptile's basking light will provide most or all the heating you need in the vivarium. In other cases, you will have to provide supplemental heating.

Most reptiles need an air temperature between 70°F and 85°F (21°C and 29.5°C) for the majority of the year. This is a bit warmer than most humans enjoy, especially if you like an air conditioner. Very few herps like a constantly warm temperature throughout their vivaria—they want cool areas and warm areas, much as you would find in nature. To provide this, try to put a heater or a basking light at one end of the vivarium, leaving the opposite end cool. This is the

A turtle basks under a ceramic heat emitter, which provides heat without light.

much-heralded concept of thermal gradient, and it really works. Many herps like the temperature to drop by five to ten degrees Fahrenheit (about three to six degrees Celsius) at night, as in nature. Heating a vivarium can be expensive, so don't set up your cage in the coolest part of the house. If you can put it in a room where the temperature stays at about 75°F (24°C) during the day, you'll save a lot on electricity.

Undertank Heaters

The most efficient vivarium heaters now available are thin plates of plastic with a heating element built into the material. These plates are designed to go under one corner of the vivarium, outside the cage, and often are held in place with glue or Velcro strips. Two basic types are available. In the cheapest and most common type, the heater maintains a temperature about five to ten degrees above the temperature in the room. This works well if you have a warm room, but it can be dangerous on hot summer days or exceptionally cold winter days, when the vivarium will become too hot or stay too cold even with the heater on. The other type of heater maintains a constant temperature, usually near 100°F (38°C). Both types are capable of producing temperatures in excess of 120°F (49°C) if they malfunction.

Undertank heaters are moderately expensive, especially in the larger sizes. They work best with glass-bottomed aquariums, as wood and plastic are poor conductors of heat. They should not be used with most types of plastic, which

An undertank electric heat plate under one corner of a vivarium allows the animal to thermoregulate.

Have an electrician
set up heat strips or
cables. Improperly
installed, they can
cause fires.

might melt. Overall, they are relatively safe and practical heaters. Remember that they go outside the vivarium and never inside unless you want to risk burning your herp.

Heating Strips

Not widely used in the United States but popular in Europe are heating cables or strips. These are flexible heating elements embedded in round, plastic tubes or flat pieces of plastic that look like gigantic strips of photographic film. Some heating cables are prewired. These often are sold in garden supply centers and now are available in pet supply

Although heat rocks
offer an additional
source of warmth,
they can cause burns
and are generally not
recommended.

shops for use with reptiles. Most heating strips, however, just have exposed contacts at the end and require individual wiring to a cord and plug. Heating strips and some cables can be cut to length to fit the vivarium and then wired for use. This is the usual method of heating snake drawer units with multiple shallow drawers. If you are not familiar with wiring, be safe and get an electrician to do the work for you.

Cables and strips tend to warm up to a fixed temperature and then stop, but occasionally they overheat and melt, causing fires. It is especially dangerous if you have to wire them yourself, unless you are very good at doing your own electrical work. Strips are easily cut, bent, or broken in everyday use, leading to short circuits and sometimes fires. Caution is advised. Consult an electrician when using heat strips or cables in units that are not prewired.

Rheostats

Most vivarium heaters slowly warm up to a preset temperature and stay at roughly the same temperature when plugged in. They do not come with any way of controlling their temperatures. To do this, you need a rheostat, a simple little device into which the heater plugs. To control the temperature in the heater, you increase or decrease the electrical resistance. Rheostats are relatively expensive but well worth the money. Don't waste your money on a cheap, low-power model; buy a good rheostat that is well made and reliable and offers you a good range of resistances.

Heat Rocks

At best, heat rocks can be used as supplemental heat for some desert lizards that get their heat both by basking in the sun and from reflected heat from the sand. A heat rock, available under many different names, is basically a plaster or resin block with a heating element buried within. Most are small, less than a foot long, and may reach temperatures well over 120°F (49°C) at one small spot on the surface. They supply heat strictly to the belly of the reptile and are not efficient at warming the air. They can also cause severe burns on the stomachs of reptiles, which cannot always sense when they are being burned. Older model heat rocks

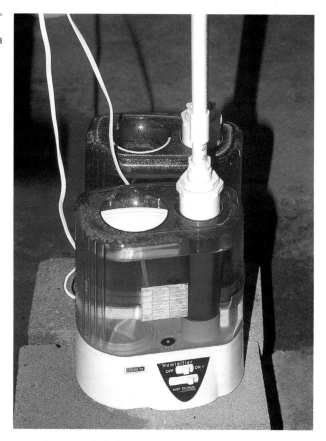

sometimes exploded when exposed to sprayed water or overheated almost to the point of melting, but modern units are much safer. Use a heat rock if you wish, but it is not recommended.

Cooling

Many amphibians are uncomfortable at temperatures above 70°F (21°C) and have to be cooled. You also must provide cool conditions for many reptiles if you plan to breed them the next season. You can cool a small vivarium by simply misting it regularly and blowing air over it with a small fan, like a primitive air conditioner. If you avoid drafts by covering the vivarium, you can also cool a vivarium by simply running an air conditioner over it, but this becomes expensive and may lead to respiratory problems. Installing an artificial waterfall with moving water often significantly cools a vivarium. Waterfall units, complete with pumps and attractive rocklike pathways for the water, are widely available at shops and over the Internet.

Probably the most efficient, but certainly not least expensive, way of keeping amphibians cool over a long period is to invest in a small refrigerator of the type used in college dorm rooms and offices. These little refrigerators usually maintain a temperature of above 40°F (5°C) when set on low. If you remove part of the seal around the door, you can easily set it to hold about 50°F (10°C) for long periods. The cost of electricity for using this method is high but generally less than trying to run an air conditioner at its lowest setting all the time.

For short-term cooling during exceptionally warm periods, you can place a small vivarium in a Styrofoam box (with a lid), and pack bags of ice or gel ice packs around it. Even just placing a sealed bag of ice on a plate within the vivarium can easily drop the temperature by five or ten degrees Fahrenheit.

Thermometers and Hygrometers

You must have at least one, but preferably two, thermometers in every vivarium, and you must keep an eye on the temperature. The best and most practical thermometers are the small electronic units that use external sensors. These are light, accurate, and inexpensive; a number of them even keep a record of maximum and minimum temperatures from day to day. Some lizards will bite through the thin wire leading to the sensor, so try to place this completely out of reach or in a small PVC plastic pipe, if necessary. The worst thermometers are the small plastic strips that glue to the side of the vivarium; they seldom are accurate, can't be placed in a good position to measure important temperatures, and don't last for more than a year or two.

Place the thermometer or its sensor near the basking area if the vivarium has one or over the undertank heater to measure the highest temperature in the cage. Another thermometer or sensor should be placed in the coolest corner so you have an idea of how much variation there is in temperature across the vivarium. Remember that you want a gradient, not a box that is always hot. Check the thermometers at least twice a day. If you try to use an aquarium thermometer, be sure that it measures in a reasonable vivarium range, from 60°F to 120°F (16°C to 49°C), and not the smaller range measured for most aquariums.

Hygrometers measure relative humidity, an indicator of how much water is present in the air. Once expensive and hard to find, hygrometers now are common and inexpensive, although they are not necessarily very accurate. You can find them as separate units that look much like dial thermometers and also as part of some electronic thermometer units. Most vivaria need a humidity range of 50 to 80 percent relative humidity, although with some desert lizards and tortoises you may want readings as low as 20 percent. Be sure the hygrometer reads a full range from 0 to 100 percent relative humidity.

Safety

The equipment mentioned in this chapter produces heat, often at very high temperatures, and some of it mixes water and electricity. Be sure that all equipment you buy is well made, preferably bears a UL (Underwriters Laboratory—a group that certifies that electrical and other equipment is safe and does what it is supposed to do) or equivalent label to assure it is at least electrically safe, and has instructions on how to connect and use it correctly. House fires, with deaths, have resulted from hot basking lights overturning or heating strips melting. Heat rocks have exploded when touched with water droplets. Iguanas have chewed into electrical cords and short-circuited everything, including themselves. There probably is no perfectly safe way to heat and light a vivarium, but you greatly reduce the chances of accidents if you use the best available equipment, make sure it stays in good working condition, and pay attention to what you are doing. If possible, never leave hot basking lights unattended for long periods of time, and certainly never let an iguana, cat, or dog roam around a room where a basking light is in use.

CHAPTER 5

TOOLS FOR THE HERP KEEPER

E very vivarium keeper needs a certain number of essential tools that make working with herps easier and safer. These include hooks and tongs for handling larger snakes and lizards, shields for safety with larger snakes, a variety of tongs or forceps for helping with feeding, and brushes and other cleaning tools. It also doesn't hurt to have a few basic veterinary tools on hand for emergencies. You don't want to go overboard with gadgets, but investing in at least a few of these items will make your life a lot easier and the hobby more enjoyable.

Safety First

Almost any herp will occasionally bite (even turtles and tortoises, and—surprisingly—a few frogs—such as horned frogs, genus *Ceratophrys*). It's especially common for a herp

A cautious keeper uses a snake hook to handle an aggressive snake.

to bite when you surprise it by trying to remove it from the vivarium or disturb it while it is sleeping. No matter how careful you are, accidents are likely to happen, and you will be nipped. This is of little consequence with most herps, but if you keep larger snakes or lizards, you certainly need some tools to allow safer handling.

Hooks

If you keep any snake more than 3 feet (91 cm) long, you need a snake hook. This simple tool consists of a curved piece of metal attached to a sturdy handle. Most hooks have a gap of about 3 to 5 inches (7.5 to 12.5 cm) between the base and tip of the hook. The tip of the hook (which is rounded and won't hurt the snake) is slowly placed under the snake at midbody, and the snake is gently lifted from the floor. This keeps the snake a bit off balance as it tries to flow along the hook and allows you to safely grasp it behind the head or just carefully transfer it to a holding container.

Snake hooks come in a variety of sizes.

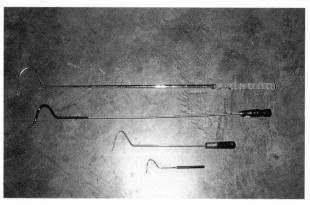

Hooks are the best way to approach and first touch any snake, including harmless specimens such as corn snakes and kingsnakes. If you simply reach into the vivarium and grab a resting corn snake around the middle, it will be surprised and may reach around and bite. The hook doesn't seem to disturb snakes as much as a hand. The hook can also be used to gently press the head and neck of an aggressive snake to the floor while you get a secure grip behind its jaws.

When you handle a snake, first grasp it behind the head even when its body is being lifted by a hook. With small and harmless specimens, you can just place your thumb alongside the head behind the base of the jaw, with your index finger against the other side of the head. With larger, nervous, or dangerous snakes, more care is essential. Place your thumb on top of the head while the rest of your hand curls around the base of the head behind the jaws. This prevents the snake from turning its head and biting. Many snakes are difficult to handle and much stronger than you might imagine. If in doubt about a snake, use only a hook and tongs.

For smaller snakes, the most convenient hook is a 7-inch (17.6 cm) adjustable pocket hook, which looks like a steel pen ending in a hook. The sections of the hook handle telescope into the base and can be extended as much as 2 feet (61 cm). These little hooks are sturdy and will easily handle something as large as a heavy adult pine snake (*Pituophis melanoleucas*) that weighs several pounds (kilos). At full extension, however, the hook tends to twist more than is safe.

Larger snake hooks commonly have a handle about 3 feet (91 cm) long made of steel, wood, or fiberglass. The hook is comparatively larger and often is flattened rather than round. Some are collapsible for easier storage. Such hooks work well with small to medium pythons and anacondas and also are used with venomous snakes. (*Warning*: venomous snakes should never be kept by beginners or those without proper experience and permits!) For the truly large snakes, special hooks with very wide gaps between the base and tip of the hook are available, but they are more likely to be sold in zoo supply catalogs than in pet shops.

Always have a hook with you when dealing with snakes and larger lizards, not only when taking them out of the vivarium to handle them but also when doing such mundane tasks as feeding and cleaning. Snakes can be unpredictable and excitable when your hand enters their space. The hook helps keep them away without increasing their excitement. Keep a small adjustable hook in your pocket at all times when working with even tame pet snakes.

Tongs

Developed from the extension tool once used in grocery stores to retrieve cans from high shelves, tongs are hollow metal tubes (now usually strong aluminum) from 2 to almost 4 feet (61 to 122 cm) long that have a pistol grip and trigger at the base and fixed and movable "fingers" at the other end. A metal cable connects the trigger to the movable fingers, allowing you to grasp a dangerous snake or lizard safely around the body from a distance. In some models, the fingers are covered with rubber or a soft plastic sleeve to reduce the chance of injury to the herp, but all good tongs have smooth surfaces on the fingers that are gentle on the animal, even without a sleeve. Avoid poorly made tongs, ones on which you can see raised seams or jagged bits of metal on the fingers. So far, tongs made of plastic have failed to be strong enough or trustworthy enough to be used with dangerous snakes. Long tongs often have a screw collar at about midlength that allows them to be folded to a more convenient length for storage.

Tongs generally are used in conjunction with hooks. The tongs grasp the snake or lizard around midbody while the hook holds down the head until the animal can be safely gripped. They also are used to collect snakes in the wild, to retrieve snakes from overhead positions in corners of large vivaria, and to move snakes from a vivarium to a holding container during cage cleaning. Tongs are essential if you have large, dangerous snakes such as pythons or venomous species, and they can be very handy when dealing with many monitors (genus *Varanus*), tegus (genus *Tupinambis*), or even aggressive green iguanas (*Iguana*).

Snake tongs allow keepers to move dangerous snakes and lizards from a distance.

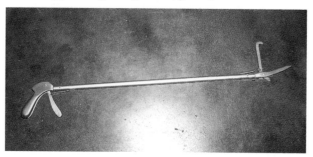

Often, you must remove a herp from its vivarium while cleaning messes or making changes to the decorations. In the case of smaller herps, this is not much of a problem as they can be stored in a critter carrier of suitable size. Snakes and lizards can be placed in a secure snake bag (such as a pillow case) tied around the top. But what do you do with a cantankerous tegu or a large python? Having a large backup vivarium just isn't practical. Instead, use a plastic garbage can with a capacity of more than 30 gallons (114 liters) and a tight-fitting lid as a holding container. Garbage cans are easy to store, inexpensive, and hard to destroy. The vertical sides prevent most larger herps from climbing out, and the lids are easily secured by bungee cords attached around the handles and over the lid. Large snakes and lizards tend to calm down when placed in a tight, dark container. A few air holes can be drilled into the upper sides or lid. Remember that garbage cans are meant as temporary containers only—never use them to hold a reptile for more than an hour or two. Place a marker (such as a red or white handkerchief) around the handle of a garbage can that is currently holding a snake or lizard to prevent anyone from accidentally opening a can.

Shields

If you plan to keep a large python or anaconda or have large monitor lizards, a shield is an essential piece of equipment. Nothing is spookier than when a large, aggressive snake or lizard makes a snap at your face. Even though contact seldom happens, it's just scary. One way to prevent these attacks (most are probably territorial challenges or threats without true malice) is to use a shield. This is simply a piece of thick, transparent plastic or Plexiglas about a foot (30 cm) wide and 18 inches (46 cm) high, with a handle affixed near the middle.

To use, you hold the shield between your face and the snake with one hand while you reach into the cage with the other. Because the shield is transparent, it allows you to keep an eye on the herp and recognize when a threat is about to start. If an attack should happen, the plastic is thick enough to protect your face as you retreat. You can also use the shield to maneuver the reptile back to its corner.

To make your own shield, bolt a metal screen door pull
onto a suitable piece of plastic. Fancier commercially made
shields also are available.

Forceps

Every herp keeper needs a few pairs of forceps around the
house. *Forceps* is just a fancy scientific term for what most
people call tweezers. In this case, however, the tweezers are
very large—well over 6 inches (15 cm) long. Hemostats are
surgical forceps shaped much like scissors, but they end in
forceps tips rather than cutting blades; hemostats usually
can be locked into several different closed and partially
closed positions. Use forceps or hemostats to offer food to
herps, pull off ticks, gently nudge small herps from their
hiding places, and even remove reluctant pieces of skin left
after the shed.

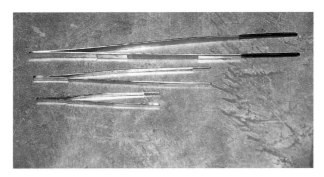

Forceps come in handy for a variety of purposes, including offering food.

You need at least two pairs of forceps. Buy one pair of slender, stainless steel forceps about 8 inches (20 cm) long, with rounded (blunt) points. Use this pair to offer bits of food to small snakes, lizards, and frogs and to help remove skin left after bad sheds. The other pair should be heavier and larger, 12 to 16 inches (30 to 40 cm) long, with an alignment spike about halfway up the prongs to make sure the tips of the blades close correctly. Use this pair to offer larger food to larger herps and to maneuver reluctant herps from behind decorations and hiding places. The tips of the forceps must be rounded, never pointed, and ridged on the insides to help grip food items. Avoid forceps that have sharp teeth at the ends—these will severely damage a herp.

Forceps and hemostats are sold at some pet supply shops and through some supply catalogs. However, buy a good grade that comes from a medical supply store. These may be more expensive, but they will last forever, and you will have a much wider selection. Forceps come in straight and curved models; get the type that feels best in your hand.

Medical Tools

Leave medical problems up to a competent veterinarian or more experienced hobbyist. There really is no need for you to buy or use most types of surgical or veterinary tools. However, there are instances in which your veterinarian may recommend force-feeding a herp or in which you must correctly deliver premeasured doses of medicines to your larger reptiles. In such cases, you will need feeding syringes and similar items.

A feeding syringe is a large-barreled syringe that does not end in a needle but instead uses a blunt tube (called a cannula) or a catheter, a piece of special plastic tubing with the opening placed slightly before the closed, rounded tip. Usually, a semiliquid food mixture, often consisting of an egg with vitamin and mineral supplements or a gelatin-based special mix, is placed in the barrel of the syringe and slowly delivered into the back of the mouth through the cannula. The herp then swallows it while the mouth is held closed. In more complicated force-feeding procedures, the catheter is inserted down the esophagus of the herp (making sure food is not aspirated into the lung or lungs) a considerable length toward the stomach, and the food is forced out of the tube through the opening just above the blunt end (to prevent injury). Forced-feeding can be dangerous to your pet—if not done correctly, the procedure can kill it. Learn forced-feeding from a veterinarian or accomplished keeper, and don't take any chances. Forced-feedings are strictly for extreme emergency situations and always should be supervised by a veterinarian.

Some shops and suppliers sell feeding syringes, catheters, and cannulas for use with reptiles. However, if your veterinarian determines that force-feeding is necessary, he or she should provide the proper equipment for you. Never force-feed your pet without consulting with your veterinarian first.

Syringes such as this one are used to administer medicine or force-feed an animal. Never force-feed your pet without first consulting a veterinarian.

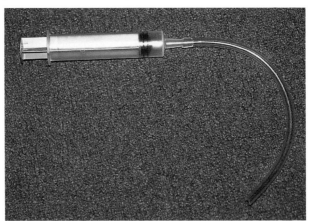

Cleaning Tools

Keeping a vivarium and its accessories clean can be time consuming, but it doesn't have to be difficult. The first thing to remember is that, unless your veterinarian specifically recommends a safe cleanser such as Roccal, nothing should be used in the vivarium except clean water and vinegar. Water and vinegar, used in conjunction with common household chlorine bleach for soaking items outside the vivarium, can keep everything clean and safe. Don't use soaps or detergents on anything that will come into contact with your herp—they may contain additives that are dangerous. This is true even of mild dish soaps. Never use antibacterial soaps on or near reptiles as the long-term effects of the antibiotic ingredients are uncertain. Clean warm water will remove almost any mess from the vivarium, and vinegar will remove many mineral deposits and leave no residue. No matter what you use, never clean the vivarium with the herps present. Even vinegar fumes can be dangerous, so remove your pets to holding containers.

Never wash reptile accessories in a sink or a bathtub used by humans—bacterial contamination is possible. Instead, purchase plastic or rubber buckets for use with your herps, and label them strictly for that. Don't use these buckets in the garden or for other tasks; chemicals residues could be dangerous to your pets, especially amphibians.

Use common household kitchen brushes to help you get all the mess and deposits off rough surfaces in the vivarium and accessories. Buy two or three different sizes so you can easily reach into any corner. Use disposable dishcloths to

A keeper cleans his cage furniture with a household brush. For small areas, a toothbrush can be used.

clean smooth surfaces. Throw them away after one use. To clean feces and urine deposits off smooth plastic, soak the area in a 1:1 solution of water and vinegar; if this doesn't work, move to straight vinegar. If this still doesn't work, carefully scrape the surface using an aquarium cleaning tool with a single-edge razor blade mounted at the end of a handle. Unfortunately, razor blades will damage plastic cages, so you may have to settle for a vinegar-clean, but still visible, smudge. Razor blade tools on longer handles allow you to clean glass surfaces that are hard to reach.

Vinegar and bleach will clean and disinfect the vivarium and its contents and tools. Regular household white vinegar is inexpensive and can be used straight or in a 1:1 vinegar to water solution. Household chlorine bleach is much more dangerous, as the sodium hypochlorite and other compounds in it can burn skin and cause severe respiratory problems. Bleaches usually are diluted to 1:1 bleach to water (strongest usable solution) or 1:9 (weakest) with water. Soak utensils and accessories in the bleach solution for one to six hours. The effectiveness of bleach in killing bacteria depends on how long the solution stays in contact with a surface as well as the strength of the solution. Just spraying a dirty surface and then wiping it or soaking it in water will seldom kill the bacteria. Plan to soak anything dirty for at least an hour before rinsing, rinsing, rinsing until all chlorine smell is gone.

You can delay cleaning of a vivarium (but not avoid it entirely) by spot cleaning and picking up feces and other messes as soon as they are noticed. Check the vivarium each morning and evening, and remove anything you see. Use a plastic spoon to scoop up waste (a plastic fork works well if you have a sandy substrate). Dispose of these utensils each day, and don't use them for more than one vivarium because they may spread any bacteria present.

Misters and Foggers

Every hobbyist needs a hand mister, a spray bottle that will let you provide a fine mist of tepid water for your animals each day. Even desert lizards, which seldom or never drink water from a dish, may need misting, drinking only condensation on their skin and on rocks. Plastic misting bottles are cheap and easy to find, but the metal bottles used for orchids and similar plants are better and last longer. Be sure to clearly mark the bottle as "water" so there are no mistakes involving cleaning fluids. (Always clearly mark bottles containing cleaning solutions as well.)

Misting by hand can be a chore, so manufacturers have come up with several machines for automatically providing a fine mist in the vivarium. Called misters or foggers, these machines use waterfalls and submerged pumps, air pressure, heaters, or ultrasonics to turn water from a reservoir into a fine mist. Some have timers that allow you to set how often the mist is released and have methods of controlling

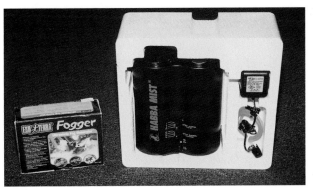

Although commercial misters are more expensive than simple spray bottles, they have several advantages, including an automatic timing system for daily mistings.

the maximum humidity in the vivarium. Waterfalls, which use a submerged pump to pass a trickle of water down a plastic "cliff face," are perhaps the most natural misters, and they increase the comfort of many forest herps and beautify the vivarium. Ultrasonic misters produce a thick fog of water vapor that tends to stay near the unit and not disperse over the vivarium unless a small fan is used.

There are complicated misting units available for use in chameleon cages that are similar to the misting units used in the vegetable section of your supermarket. A narrow nozzle at the end of a plastic tube allows water under pressure to turn into a fine mist that is dispersed over the vivarium. These units, which may be simple and inexpensive (basically a bottle holding water and a pump to push it through the nozzle) or quite complicated and very expensive (with timers, variable pressures and pump settings, even heaters to provide a warm mist), seldom are sold in pet supply shops but are easy to find in mail-order catalogs and on the Internet. Their major problem is that hard-water deposits quickly clog the nozzle, so it must be constantly cleaned or replaced unless you use distilled water. Heavy misting also cools a vivarium.

Putting It All Together

Once you've gotten all your equipment together, you are ready to actually set up your vivarium. Unfortunately, there are no set rules, and a lot has to do with what type of herp you are going to keep. You cannot keep a salamander as you would a corn snake or an iguana.

There are only a few basic types of vivaria. If you are a beginner, then start simply and work up to more complicated designs. There are several good books on the market that will give you lots of ideas about interesting ways to make your vivarium distinctive, but they still all rely on the basics you'll find here.

CHAPTER 6

WOODLAND VIVARIA

The woodland vivarium probably is the most familiar and widely used type of vivarium. It is fine for most nondesert herps from the United States and Europe, and it also works well with many exotic herps that don't need extreme conditions. Basically, it is a simple vivarium setup with nice-looking substrate and decorations.

Basic Setup

Woodland vivaria work well with aquarium cages and sliding-door cages of almost any size. Instead of paper on the bottom (as you would use in a sterile vivarium), use 2 inches (5 cm) or more of clean aspen or pine shavings for the bedding. Add at least one or two branches that could be used for basking or just for decoration, and put in a few artificial broad-leaved plants to make the vivarium look more natural and attractive. On top of the cage, place a full-spectrum light, a daylight white tube, and a basking light if needed. If you use a basking light, place a flat rock, piece of

This woodland setup features an aspen shaving substrate, a hide box, and a basking site.

A keeper puts down
aspen shavings for
the substrate of his
new woodland
vivarium.

cork bark, or a similar comfortable basking spot under the
light. Woodland vivaria are great displays, so you want them
to be well lit. This means that you must provide at least one
nice, natural-looking hide box per specimen so all the herps
can get away from the light if they wish. For heat, place an
undertank heater under part of the floor (no more than half
the surface), and set it to maintain a temperature of about
80°F (26.5°C).

Electronic thermometers work well in woodland vivaria
because the readout units can be positioned outside the
vivarium and the sensors placed on the basking area and in
the coolest corner to keep track of the temperature. Use a
hygrometer to be sure that you maintain the 60 to 80

The heat strip posi-
tioned under one end
(lower left) of this
cage will allow the
animal inside to
thermoregulate.

percent humidity that most woodland herps require. Hand-misting each day usually supplies sufficient water to maintain the humidity, especially if the artificial plants are sprayed regularly to increase evaporation.

If using a vivarium with sliding front doors, install a strip of plastic or aluminum flashing between the bedding and the rails. If shavings get into the rails, the glass will be very difficult to move, which means that you will have an excuse to not clean the vivarium as often as you should.

The Herps

Woodland vivaria make excellent displays and can be modified to house a host of different types of herps, from

A corn snake rests in its woodland vivarium. Among the most common herps kept in captivity, corn snakes do well in this type of vivarium.

corn and rat snakes (genus *Elaphe* and relatives) to Burmese pythons (*Python molurus bivittatus*), anoles, and geckos. Arboreal herps such as anoles and swifts (*Sceloporus* spp.) need more climbing areas than do herps that live on the ground, such as common skinks (genus *Eumeces* and allies); and nocturnal herps, such as most snakes, need less in the way of basking lights.

Rather surprisingly, most common chameleons (genus *Chamaeleo* and relatives) are more comfortable in a tall woodland terrarium with moderate humidity and temperature than in a hot, moist enclosed rain forest vivarium. Chameleons often do poorly when kept much above 85°F (29.5°C), except under a basking light. Although they like to

A Jamaican anole perches on a leaf in its woodland vivarium. Anoles need plants or other objects to climb.

be misted regularly and even like foggers, they seldom come from habitats that could be considered rain forest. Many are actually animals of plains and mountainsides, and they like good airflow.

Use common sense, read up on the best way to keep your pet, and then make adjustments to the vivarium to match. You can make a woodland vivarium very complicated with living plants and special lighting, but remember that complicated vivaria are harder to service and take more of your time—time that may be better devoted to working with your animals.

CHAPTER 7
RAIN FOREST VIVARIA

R ecently, there has been a growing interest in large, very tall, heavily planted vivaria that try to mimic the rain forests of the tropics. Hobbyists build walk-in cages with glass and mesh doors and provide miniature trees loaded with bromeliads, creepers, and even orchids. Somewhere in the background may be a gecko or two (day geckos [*Phelsuma* species] are frequently used) or even an iguana, but often you have to look hard to find the herps. A good rain forest vivarium, however, should accent the animals, not the plants.

Basic Setup

A rain forest vivarium can actually be quite simple and easy to develop. You need a tall cage that will support a variety of basking perches, such as old branches and pieces of driftwood. The base must be waterproof enough to withstand a constant drip of moisture. For decorations, there are a variety of artificial vines and bromeliads that

A rain forest vivarium, such as this one, requires a good drip or misting system.

You can use hardwood mulch, such as orchid bark, for a rain forest substrate.

are quite nice to look at. Their wide leaves provide a good surface for the evaporation of misted water and the increase of humidity.

For a substrate, use a variety of hardwood mulches (orchid bark) or even aspen shavings. The best beddings are those that hold water well and stay humid yet allow little growth of molds and bacteria. The herps kept in rain forest vivaria usually are climbers; some spend almost all their time on their branches, seldom coming to the ground.

You will need a basking light placed in line with a favorite branch. You also will need a fluorescent fixture holding both full-spectrum and daylight-white lights. Some rain forest herps need subdued light, but most of those kept in vivaria like bright light part of the day and

Use a tall, mesh-covered cage with a waterproof base for a rain forest setup.

Some type of misting system is almost always used in rain forest vivaria. Most herps kept in such vivaria need high humidity as well as good ventilation, as you would find among the leaves of tall trees. Just misting with a hand mister seldom works well, so most keepers use an automated system. The simplest is a drip-waterer, which basically is a water bottle sitting on top of the vivarium and fitted with a length of plastic tubing and a valve. The valve is adjusted so the water comes out as drops or a slight trickle that lands on a broad leaf or branch to increase evaporation. As the water works its way down toward the vivarium base, it evaporates from the heat and then recondenses in the pan under the vivarium. More sophisticated misting systems use pumps to force water through fine nozzles and can be adjusted to produce different amounts of mist at specific times of the day.

display brilliant colors when kept in bright light. Most are diurnal (active during the day).

The simplest rain forest vivaria perhaps are the mesh cages sold for chameleons. Place the cage over a plastic bowl or pan that will catch water passing through the cage. Limit bedding to some aspen or a thin layer of mulch to keep the bottom damp but not wet. Angle one or two branches across the cage, and add some artificial vines or living philodendrons as decoration. On top of the cage, place lights, both full-spectrum and basking, plus a

Bromeliads are the ideal plants for rain forest vivaria.

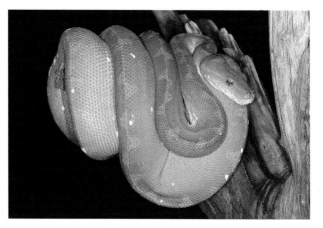

misting system or drip-waterer. Presto, you have a decent rain forest cage. These mesh cages allow adequate air circulation, which is important for many reptiles but is likely to be lacking in an enclosed rain forest vivarium. A feature that can work to increase the humidity in rain forest vivaria is a waterfall.

Rain forest vivaria allow the advanced hobbyist a great deal of variety in setting up the cage and outfitting it with decorative materials of many types. However, sometimes the keeper can't see the forest for the trees. You are trying

A red-eyed tree frog rests on a large leaf. Red-eyed tree frogs are excellent herps for a rain forest setup.

to keep reptiles and amphibians in comfortable surroundings that at least somewhat mimic their natural habitat;
you are not just trying to paint a pretty picture with plants.
That's a different hobby.

The Herps

Rain forest vivaria can vary greatly in size and complexity,
and they can accommodate a wide variety of herps, from
tropical tree frogs (*Hyla* spp.) and red-eyed tree frogs, also
called leaf-frogs (*Agalychnis callidryas* and relatives) to boas
and pythons that enjoy humid surroundings (such as green
tree pythons, *Python* [*Morelia*] *viridis*, and emerald tree
boas, *Corallus caninus*). If you restrict the humidity in parts
of the vivarium, you can keep many types of tropical day
geckos (*Phelsuma* spp.). These day-active, brightly colored
little lizards add color to any vivarium. As a rule, almost any
herp not restricted to dry plains and deserts can live in a rain
forest vivarium. Even herps from woodland habitats can live
in a rain forest vivarium, especially if you make part of the
vivarium a bit drier than the rest.

CHAPTER 8

DESERT VIVARIA

I n a desert vivarium, you are trying to keep herps (usually lizards and sometimes snakes) that come from areas that are hot during the day and usually cooler at night. Sand and rocks do not hold heat once the sun goes down. You are not trying to bake your animals. Yes, there are some herps, such as spiny-tailed lizards (genus *Uromastyx*) and desert iguanas (genus *Dipsosaurus*), that cannot thrive or even survive unless their body temperature remains above 90°F (32°C), needing temperatures of 115°F to 120°F (46°C to 49°C) to even digest their food, but they are the exceptions.

Cycles

Most desert herps have a regular rhythm of life. They get up in the morning, find a bright, sunny spot in which to bask and raise their core body temperature to about 95°F to 100°F (35°C to 38°C), and then move away from the basking area to hunt, mate, or just hang out—often in partially shaded areas. When the sun reaches its warmest, they retreat

A leopard gecko utilizes a hide box in an elaborate desert setup.

to burrows or hiding spots under rocks and logs to remain at a temperature much lower than the 105°F to 115°F (41°F to 46°C) of many desert afternoons. In fact, if you expose most desert lizards and snakes to bright, unfiltered sunlight when they are not in basking mode, they will rapidly become stressed and try to hide. If forced to stay in the light and heat, they may die in just a few minutes. In the later afternoon, the herps come out again to warm up by basking and to do some more hunting; then they retreat to their burrows to spend the night as the temperature often drops by thirty degrees Fahrenheit (seventeen degrees Celsius) or more.

However, many desert herps are nocturnal, coming out at night to feed and mate. They seldom see the sun, except for a short period at dusk and dawn. This is why herp collectors in the desert ride the roads and look for geckos and snakes at night, not during midday.

Setup

The desert vivarium is not a hot box but a vivarium with relatively dry bedding, a hot basking area available if the herps want it, and cooler places to retreat for resting.

Most desert vivaria contain a mixture of sand and a bit of potting soil for bedding because it is easy to keep clean and many herps find it natural and comfortable. The soil makes it easier for burrows to stay formed; pure sand will just collapse. Of course, sand tends to escape from a cage with

To avoid sand spillage, use a top-opening aquarium for a desert vivarium.

For a cleaner, nicer looking substrate, a keeper adds soil to the sand in his vivarium.

doors at the front, so this limits your choice of cages to those that open from the top. You can also have a high lip at the front to control spreading sand, although this seldom works 100 percent of the time. The bedding should be at least 2 inches (5 cm) thick, but 4 inches (10 cm) thick is not out of the question. Rocks, cork bark, and bits of wood help form the decor and also give the herps places to start burrows. Few living plants do well in desert vivaria (you will find cacti very hard to keep alive), but there are some excellent artificials that look great.

Most desert reptiles like dry conditions, so restrict the water bowl to a small one. With some herps, such as desert iguanas (genus *Dipsosaurus*) and sand boas (genus *Eryx*), it

Use artificial cacti in desert vivaria. Herps can injure themselves on the spines of real cacti.

is best to give water only once or twice a week, although few are as delicate (immediately reacting poorly to excess humidity) as some keepers believe. Some burrowing desert lizards (barrel skinks [genus *Chalcides*], for instance) do best with a light daily misting and a bit of water poured down two corners of the vivarium every week to assure at least two humid spots under the surface when wanted. The humidity in a desert vivarium should be held between perhaps 10 and 30 percent, with good ventilation. You will need a hygrometer and the usual pair of thermometers or sensors in the hot and cold spots.

A desert setup requires both full-spectrum and basking lights.

Do not keep the sand of the entire vivarium hot, just a spot under the basking light. Remember that most desert herps escape the heat of the day by burrowing into the cooler ground. This makes using an undertank heater tricky, as it would make the ground warmer than wanted by most desert herps, especially at night. You can think of a desert vivarium in three sections: one very hot section under the basking light, one warm section close to the basking light over an undertank heater, and the rest of the vivarium unheated and cool at night.

Timers will help you control the basking light (on for about eight hours a day), the full-spectrum and daylight-fluorescent lights (on about twelve hours a day), and the undertank heater (for most herps set for about 80°F [26.5°C] during the day and turned off or down at night).

Many desert lizards like to climb, so decorate the vivarium with groups of rocks or pieces of weathered driftwood. Glue rocks together with silicone cement, and attach them to the base of the vivarium to prevent collapse in case a lizard jostles or undermines the stack.

Comments on Plants

The obvious choice of plants for a desert vivarium is cacti, right? Wrong. Cacti, with few exceptions, are difficult plants to grow in a desert vivarium, even when kept in pots. They have delicate root systems and are easily damaged by excess humidity or the attentions of a passing lizard. Most specimens sold at low prices in variety stores and general nurseries fail to thrive, even with the best of care; usually they survive for only a few weeks. In addition, most cacti have spines that can injure a lizard perching on it or passing nearby. This may seem odd, as lizards often live in cactus thickets in nature, but there they have a larger area in which to move about and can avoid spines more easily than in a vivarium.

Many succulents, such as the smaller succulent African euphorbs (genus *Euphorbia* and relatives) and small species of *Gasteria* and *Haworthia* with wedge-shaped leaves (or stems in some cases—but don't worry too much about the details of their botany), survive better in a desert vivarium.

Succulents are the best plants for a desert setup.

They do especially well when potted and replaced at regular intervals with fresh plants and given a chance to rest outside of the vivarium. Snake plants (*Sansevieria* species) of the right size to fit the vivarium also do well and are not easily injured by lizards or a bit of condensation.

Remember that excellent imitations of desert plants are available today, ones that look as good as the real plants. You also won't have to worry about spines, black spots from condensation, or gnawing by lizards.

Desert Herps

This chuckwalla basks on a warm rock. All desert species require a warm, low-humidity environment.

Desert herps, especially lizards, are widely sold, and many do well in a vivarium if the humidity is kept low. Some specialized lizards, such as uromastyx, spiny-tailed agamids (genus *Uromastyx*), and chuckwallas (genus *Sauromalus*), can digest their food only when their body temperature is over 100°F (38°C). Humid surroundings lead to lingering death. Leopard geckos (*Eublepharis macularius*), however, and a few day geckos (such as *Phelsuma standingi*) are typical desert lizards that are hardy enough to survive even when the humidity rises. Few desert lizards are hardier than the common bearded dragon (*Pogona vitticeps*), one of the most popular herps sold today. Many small lizards from the deserts of North America (such as swifts [genus *Sceloporus*], racerunners [genus *Cnemidophorus* and relatives], and earless lizards [genus *Holbrookia*]) are collected from the wild and sold as pets. They usually have to be dewormed and slowly acclimated to life in the vivarium. It is always safest and most environmentally sound to purchase captive-bred specimens when available.

Among snakes, the sand boas (genus *Eryx*) and rosy boas (*Lichanura trivirgata*) are at home in dry surroundings. Some of the African and Asian sand boas may never see rain in their natural habitats. Other snakes that may do well in dry vivaria include such species as common kingsnakes (*Lampropeltis getula*) and many desert racers and whipsnakes (genera *Coluber* and *Masticophis*).

Tortoises are often inhabitants of desert conditions, although their size in many cases prevents them from being kept in simple vivaria. Texas gopher tortoises (*Gopherus berlandieri*) and desert gopher tortoises (*Gopherus agassizii*) do well when small, as do baby leopard and African spurred tortoises (*Geochelone pardalis* and *Geochelone sulcata*), but all will outgrow even a large vivarium in a few years. Remember that most tortoises are protected by law, especially those of the United States. It is simply illegal to pick up any species of gopher tortoise (genus *Gopherus*) other than to rescue it by moving it to the other side of the road. Be sure that your specimens have been legally caught or bred.

A desert rosy boa will thrive in a desert vivarium.

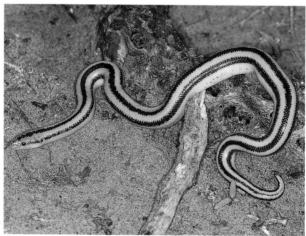

Some amphibians, such as this Couch's spadefoot toad, are appropriate for desert vivaria.

Even amphibians are not complete strangers to the desert, or at least dry savannas or prairies, as some toads (genus *Bufo*) adapt well to dry conditions and live for years with just an occasional misting. Spadefoot toads (genus *Scaphiopus*) are common inhabitants of North American deserts and can be kept in quite dry surroundings. African bullfrogs (genus *Pyxicephalus*) also thrive in dry conditions if occasionally allowed to soak.

CHAPTER 9

WET VIVARIA

The boundaries between vivaria and aquariums are indistinct and constantly shifting. Many keepers maintain 50-gallon (190-liter) aquariums with a few fish but also some aquatic turtles, such as small red-eared sliders (*Trachemys scripta elegans*) or aquatic salamanders. The only concession to the vivarium in such a setup is a plastic ramp that allows the turtles to leave the water to bask under a basking light. In a so-called aqua-vivarium, about half the cage is devoted to a body of water that is filtered and heated and half to a moist land area, the two often grading into each other. For this book's purposes, if it needs a filter, it is an aquarium, not a vivarium.

A wet vivarium, by contrast, is a cage, usually an aquarium because an aquarium can withstand the constant high humidity and water. Sometimes, though, you can use a sturdy plastic or rubber tub if it has a constantly moist bedding area, usually is kept quite cool, and generally houses some living mosses. These are the vivaria often used for small frogs such as poison dart frogs (genus *Dendrobates*

A frog soaks in a wet vivarium. Wet setups for amphibians require full-spectrum lighting but not basking lights.

There is a fine line between an aquarium and a wet vivarium. This is a wet vivarium for a water turtle.

and relatives), mantellas, and tree frogs—as well as woodland salamanders and mostly terrestrial newts.

Basic Setup

Start with a water-tight cage, such as a 10- or 20-gallon (38- or 76-liter) aquarium. With amphibians, smaller vivaria often work better than larger ones and are easier to keep clean. It's also easier to keep an eye on your pets in a small vivarium. The lid can be the usual metal mesh, but you don't need a metal rim because you won't be using a basking light. (You can suspend a full-spectrum fluorescent fixture over the cage by letting the fixture sit on the frame. It's cool and shouldn't warp a plastic cage frame.) Because it is

To create a wet vivarium, you must start with a water-tight aquarium, such as the one shown here.

A plastic sheet under one area of the mesh increases the vivarium's humidity.

important to keep the humidity in the cage high, many keepers use a solid lid, such as a sheet of heavy plastic or even glass. Solid lids, however, prevent ventilation, and the wet vivarium rapidly becomes dank, with bacterial and fungal colonies growing everywhere. Instead, use a regular mesh lid, and cut a sheet of plastic to fit under the lid. Use the translucent heavy plastic that is made to seal windows during the winter or the type used for painter drop cloths. Cut the plastic wide enough to hang over the edges of the vivarium when the lid is in place. By moving the plastic sheet so it covers more or less of the vivarium top, you can increase or decrease the humidity. Use a small fan to blow air across the top of the vivarium from a distance of at least a foot. This helps increase ventilation without causing drafts.

Cover the bottom of the vivarium with an inch or two (2.5 to 5 cm) of clean, uniform, small pea gravel. The type used in aquariums is fine, but colors are not necessary; you won't notice the gravel in a few days. To make sure that the gravel is dust free, put it in a bucket and run water through it until the water flowing out is clean. Don't trust labels—prewashed gravel often is loaded with dirt and dust. On top of the gravel, add a layer of living moss, the type you find for sale in the pet supply shop. Such moss is not always alive, but it holds its shape and colors for long periods. It also absorbs a lot of water. Live sphagnum moss, which is sold as a separate product from forest moss, is said to produce chemicals that control the growth of bacteria, which helps keep the bedding sanitary. Be prepared to replace some or all the moss every month, especially if you are keeping frogs. They are dirty animals and hard on the bedding.

If you want to get more complicated, you can drill a drain hole in one corner of the cage and fit it with a length of hose and a pinch-cock or valve. This allows you to use a misting machine that regularly sprays the vivarium with fine droplets of water. The excess water will accumulate in the bottom gravel of the aquarium, where it normally would become a mess, but the drain lets you easily clean it out every week. If you use a hand mister two or three times a day (all that most amphibians really need), you will only have to change the vivarium monthly.

Waterfalls

The best way of adding some life and distinction to a wet vivarium (or to a rain forest vivarium, for that matter) is to

For substrate, cover 2 inches of gravel with living sphagnum moss, as shown in this side view of a wet vivarium.

111

add a simple waterfall. Until recently, this was difficult, requiring knowledge of water pressures from pump heads and a lot of trial and error to get the rate of water flow over the vertical surface of the waterfall just right. Return pipes often got clogged and vivaria flooded, a disaster from any viewpoint.

Today, however, you can purchase premade waterfall kits that can be fitted to aquariums between 10 and 50 gallons (38 and 190 liters) in size. The kits typically consist of a molded plastic surface for the waterfall and a streamlike channel ending in a drain. A simple pump inside the waterfall continuously pulls water from the drain area back to the waterfall and releases it at a sufficient pressure to make a nice display. These kits usually work very well, seldom flood, and don't require advanced plumbing knowledge to put together.

The valved drains connected to these wet vivaria allow for easy cleaning.

This large, elaborate wet setup includes living plants and a waterfall.

There are two major advantages of a waterfall. One is its looks—even the smallest waterfall adds a natural feeling to the vivarium. More important, moving water increases the humidity in the air of the vivarium, which allows you to easily keep small amphibians such as poison dart frogs and tree frogs as well as salamanders, animals notorious for the difficulty of getting just the right humidity to suit them. Waterfall kits are widely sold in stores specializing in herps and through Internet sources. They are certainly worth a try.

Herps

Wet vivaria are best for frogs and many salamanders. Most snakes and lizards will quickly develop bacterial infections in the belly scales that could lead to death. Many frogs, however, thrive in a mossy vivarium with a waterfall and very high humidity. Much has been written on designing vivaria for the multitude of poison frogs (genera *Dendrobates*, *Epipedobates*, and *Phyllobates*) and mantellas (genus *Mantella*) that sport brilliant colors and often have strange breeding habitats. Such frogs seldom thrive in a simple vivarium, usually doing well only in elaborately decorated naturalistic vivaria. In fact, keeping these frogs has developed into a specialized side branch of herpetoculture.

Salamanders are the neglected herps, seldom collected for the vivarium, seldom sold, and seldom bred in captivity. The wet vivarium is the best habitat for many salamanders,

as most require moist surroundings and dislike dry air. Fire salamanders (*Salamandra salamandra*) from Europe sometimes are available, their bright black and red patterns adding life to any vivarium, but don't neglect the occasional North American mole salamanders (genus *Ambystoma*) and dusky salamanders (genus *Desmognathus*) that appear in shops seasonally. Few herps are more attractive than the black and yellow tiger salamander (*Ambystoma tigrinum*) or spotted salamander (*Ambystoma maculatum*), while the delicate silvery pattern of a marbled salamander (*Ambystoma opacum*) is sure to draw attention. Most salamanders are secretive and seldom come out except at night, so use a red or blue light in the vivarium at night so you can observe your salamanders' activities without disturbing them.

This spotted salamander rests on lush greenery in a wet vivarium. Although salamanders are rarely collected for keeping, they make excellent pets.

CHAPTER 10
OUTDOOR VIVARIA

U nlike the other types of vivaria discussed here, outdoor vivaria, as a rule, are do-it-yourself enclosures.
Unless you can purchase a large iguana cage and
mount it on wheels to take outdoors on nice days
(which some hobbyists will do), you need to build
your own outdoor vivarium.

Is It Practical?

Before deciding to spend the time and labor (as well as
money) to make an outdoor enclosure, carefully consider
whether your pet really needs to be outdoors and whether it
can tolerate your local weather. Outdoor enclosures generally are used for turtles and tortoises that require large areas
in which to roam and for larger lizards (green iguanas, tegus,
and some monitors) that require large quarters and do best
when allowed to bask under natural sunlight. They also are
used for smaller lizards, such as anoles and chameleons, that
need nonstagnant air as well as some sunlight.

A keeper constructs
an outdoor cage, a
relatively quick and
easy project. Outdoor
cages for smaller
lizards are often
made to hang from
trees.

The problem is that weather seldom is constant. In many places, both the temperature and the humidity are subject to sudden rapid fluctuations. Unless your home is in the sub-tropics or tropics, where temperatures are relatively constant much of the year, you must be alert for changes in weather and have a safe place to take your pet in from outdoors. My state of Louisiana, for instance, is a place that many people believe has fairly constant temperatures. The reality is that during late summer the temperature may reach over 95°F (35°C) for many days in a row, and beginning in mid-October nighttime temperatures start to drop below 50°F (10°C). Winter temperatures commonly are below 40°F at night for several months. In Louisiana and most other southern states, all herps must come indoors by the end of October, even large tortoises, which do not do well at low nighttime temperatures. This means, for example, that each evening my 30-pound (13.5-kilo) African spurred tortoise (*Geochelone sulcata*) has to come indoors and be placed in a 100-gallon (380-liter) tub, then taken out the next day if the temperature and sunlight are suitable for basking. Central American wood turtles (*Rhinoclemmys pulcherrima*) must come indoors by the end of October and won't go out again until March or April. Box turtles (*Terrapene carolina*), by contrast, could stay outdoors for most of a Louisiana winter, but even they should be brought inside if the temperature approaches freezing for several days in a row. Louisiana keepers must maintain not only outdoor enclosures but also a variety of tubs and tanks in a heated building. This would be true in most parts of the United States and Europe.

This frequent moving of animals must be done in most parts of the world. If you want to keep many turtles and large lizards, you will have to build them outdoor quarters and be prepared to maintain them indoors for four to six months of each year.

Small Lizard Vivaria

Assuming the weather is good for your species, you can easily allow your anole, small iguana, or chameleon to get some indirect sunlight and fresh air outdoors almost any time of the year by either modifying a purchased mesh chameleon cage or building a simple mesh cage.

A keeper attaches nylon mesh around the wooden frame of an outdoor cage.

Many mesh chameleon cages that use lightweight fiberglass or PVC plastic frames are strong enough to be hung from a tree branch or even a bird cage stand in a shaded location for a few hours a day. If the cage does not already have a hanging hook attachment, make one by extending a wire across the top of the cage and twisting it in the middle to form a simple hook or hanging eye screw. Just remember that these cages are not really made for outdoor use and are light enough to really bob about in even a slight wind. They also will not survive attacks from small predators such as grackles, jays, and squirrels, so you must supervise them at all times. Don't fall asleep in your lawn chair!

Making your own simple hanging cage is easy and requires only basic tools. Plan on a base of quarter-inch or thicker plywood (to give weight and stability), and use the same material for the top. Two pieces of plywood about 2 feet (61 cm) square are satisfactory for most smaller lizards. If you purchase a half-sheet (4 feet x 4 feet [122 x 122 meters]), you can probably get two cuts for free at the lumber store. That's all you need to get enough for two cages. Furring strips of thin wood about 2 inches (5 cm) wide are used for the uprights of the cage, either stapled or nailed to the plywood at each corner. A good height is 3 feet (91 cm), which allows you to easily reach all the corners to retrieve your lizard. To enclose the cage, securely staple flexible fiberglass or aluminum window-screen material over the frame.

To thwart escapes, add a shirt-sleeve entry. Just knot the sleeve to close it.

A keeper attaches a chain to the top of the cage to complete the hanging vivarium.

For a safe, almost escape-proof door, create a sleeve door. To do this, cut out a circle about 6 inches (15 cm) in diameter near the center of one side. Now, stitch part of an old shirt sleeve about 2 feet (61 cm) long around the hole. Put the sleeve into the cage with the cuff end loosely knotted. To operate, pull the knotted sleeve out of the cage, untie it, and insert your hand and arm through the hole. It is almost impossible for the lizard to escape through the sleeve. You will find that this type of sleeve door is very safe to use when handling agile lizards that have been warmed up in the sun and jump about quickly. If you wish, you can make a more traditional door by cutting out a rectangle of mesh and replacing it with a slightly larger rectangle of mesh that overlaps the opening. It is difficult to secure such a door with wire or even Velcro without making a frame. In addition, small anoles often manage to wedge themselves between the cut edges of the mesh and wriggle out. The sleeve method is probably safer.

To hang the cage, use a hook and eye arrangement such as the one used for screen doors. Screw the eye into the center of the upper plywood panel of the cage for even weight distribution. The hook should have a safety catch on it (a simple flat piece of spring metal that is pulled out to allow it to hook into the eye) to prevent random winds from blowing the anchoring apart. Use a length of light chain to hang the cage from a branch or beam.

When you are decorating outdoor hanging lizard cages, remember that they are not made to hold lots of weight. Use artificial vines or a small branch. If you supply water through a drip-waterer outdoors, remember that even a bottle of water sitting on top of the cage may stress simple construction techniques such as staples.

Iguana Cages

If you have an adult green iguana (*Iguana iguana*), spiny-tailed iguana (*Ctenosaura* spp.), tegu (*Tupinambis* spp.), larger monitor (*Varanus* spp.), rock iguana (*Cyclura* spp.), or other large lizard, you will almost certainly want to keep it outdoors during the summer when the weather is fine. Most of these lizards are 3 feet (91 cm) long or better, can climb, are active to aggressive, and want lots of space. Breeding virtually requires a large outdoor enclosure

This spacious walk-in enclosure makes a good summer home for large lizards.

(unless you can give them their own room) because the lizards tend to chase about during courtship. Many also like to bask in bright or shaded sunlight. Putting them out in good weather for at least three to six months a year is good for them and gives the keeper a break from cleaning indoor quarters.

Two common ways of thinking about outdoor cages for large lizards are as 1) lightweight cages that can be moved about, and 2) larger fixed cages designed to hold the lizard outdoors for months at a time.

Movable Cages

If you already have purchased a large mesh or welded wire iguana cage up to about 3 feet (91 cm) deep by 6 feet (183 cm) long and 5 to 6 feet (152 to 183 cm) high, it should be a simple task to convert it into a movable cage that can be taken outdoors for a day or a week at a time. In fact, some iguana cages come with heavy bottom frames and are set up to support casters of various types. Almost any can be modified to accept wheels by cutting down a sheet of heavy outdoor plywood to fit the bottom of the cage and attaching casters to this sheet. You can also use metal bed frames, which often are adjustable to fit cages and have casters installed. Remember that most iguana cages are rectangular, so be sure to reinforce the center of the two long sides of the cage with wood or metal strips to prevent sagging.

Remember to consider the size of your doors between rooms and between house and outdoors. You don't want to spend time modifying an existing indoor cage and then find it won't fit through the door. You also want to be sure that the indoor cage is secure enough to withstand winds, light rains, and possibly even attacks from predators while you are not watching it. Stray dogs and cats are always a potential problem. If the cage is left outdoors overnight, you also may have to consider opossums, raccoons, coyotes, and similar predators—even a large city may become a jungle at night. If you are unsure about the cage's ability to withstand predators, don't take a chance—bring it in at night.

You can build your own movable iguana cage using welded wire with at least 1-inch (2.5-cm) spacing to prevent problems from snout rubbing. Be sure to brace all corners (some lizards can be very determined escape artists when exposed to natural sunlight) and especially the lower joints where the vertical supports connect to the floor. The door should be large enough for you to enter for cleaning and maintenance, yet it should latch securely at least at the top and the bottom. Consider adding a padlock to the door to prevent theft of unattended lizards. Heavy outdoor plywood makes a good floor for such a cage. The top should be made of wire. Consider covering half the top with a sheet of corrugated roofing plastic to make sure the lizard can get out of the rain.

Fixed Cages

Building a fixed cage for a large lizard can be complicated and expensive, especially when you consider that in most areas you can use the cage only for a few months each year. However, if you have a really large lizard, such as an adult male green iguana or water monitor (*Varanus salvator*), your pet will be happy and comfortable only if kept outdoors in a cage or pen that is at least 8 feet (2.4 m) wide and 8 to 16 feet (2.4 to 4.8 m) long—just big enough to let it move about easily.

Zoning

Always check with your local government to make sure that it is legal to build a fixed cage on your property. You may be surprised to find that everything that goes into the ground needs a permit, often at a fee, and that your neighbors may have a say as to whether you can build or not. Movable cages seldom require any zoning permits.

To build a fixed cage, use 4-inch x 4-inch x 8-foot (10-cm x 10-cm x 240-cm) posts at the corners, with a pair of central posts to support the frame better and to allow placement of the door. Use 2-inch x 4-inch x 8-foot (5-cm x 10-cm x 240-cm) lumber for the frame. You must use treated lumber to prevent damage from fungi and insects. However, cover all interior treated surfaces with wire to prevent the lizard from possibly chewing or licking chemically treated wood. Place braces in the corners to prevent the cage from swaying in the wind or succumbing to attacks from predators. It is easiest to drop the supporting posts into the ground at least 18 inches (46 cm) deep, leaving you over 6 feet (1.8 m) of head room.

Because you are dealing with large, strong lizards, use wire around and on top of the cage that is strong enough to resist attacks. Strong wire also protects your pet from predators. One-inch (2.5-cm) welded wire, often used for rabbit hutches, works fine and is not excessively expensive. Hexagonal mesh chicken wire is much cheaper but breaks easily, leaving loose points of wire that can severely injure both lizard and owner. Chicken wire is at best a temporary measure until you get better wire. Wire with spacing over an inch wide will allow in rats and may even let dogs and cats take swipes at a lizard with their paws.

If you can afford it, use double doors for the pen. You can build your own doors using simple wooden boards that are properly braced or buy used storm doors and rewire them with welded wire. Set the interior door flush with the rest of the pen frame and the outer door about 2 feet (61 cm) outside. Connect the outer door to the cage with a solid wood frame so that the doors can both be securely hinged into position. Double doors allow you to open the outer door, step inside the frame, close the outer door, and then open the inner door. This will prevent a lizard from making a break for the outdoors. Both doors must have secure latches, and the outer door should be lockable. If you cannot afford double doors or don't have the space (or carpentry skills) to install them, at least place a footboard in the frame of your single door. This is just a panel about 30 inches (76 cm) high (plywood or several wide boards placed one over the other) anchored across the bottom of the door. To get into the cage, you will have to step over the footboard, but it will slow most lizards down before they can scramble or jump over it. As long as you remember to check where your lizard is resting when you enter and your pet is not a notorious jumper, a footboard may be all you ever need.

This large, outdoor setup features double doors and a high threshold to prevent escapes.

Every lizard cage needs a retreat for your pet. In the case of climbing lizards (iguanas of many types), build a small enclosure (about half the length of the specimen) in one upper corner, and use a branch or primitive ladder to provide access. Enclose the retreat at top and bottom, back, and two sides. Leave the front open for easy cleaning and access. If you decide to add a heat lamp (used by many lizards on damp, dark days), be sure it is fully separated by heavy wire mesh or a considerable space from the area used by the lizard so burns are not possible. In the case of most larger monitors and tegus, which are not noted as great climbers, the enclosure can be much simpler. Place a panel about 3 feet (91 cm) high across one corner, with a roof made of wood or corrugated plastic or tin. Cut a hole in the panel so the lizard can enter and leave. Make sure the roof is easily removable so you can get in for cleaning and to check on your pet.

Remember to supply semiaquatic lizards (such as water monitors) with a suitably large bathing tub and ramps inside and out to help them get in and out of the tub. In fact, most lizards will use a bathing tub at least occasionally, and certainly it is easier to let your lizard bathe outdoors than in an indoor vivarium.

Turtle Enclosures

Even small turtles such as box turtles (*Terrapene* spp.) do best when kept outdoors part of the year. Few turtles really reach their prime when kept indoors. Turtles, especially tortoises, need natural sunlight and lots of room to roam if they are to be perfectly comfortable. You can use movable lizard cages for this or place them in fixed outdoor cages, but if you keep mostly turtles and tortoises, it is more efficient to give them their own enclosures.

Ground area is more important than height in turtle enclosures, and you want to give your pet the largest area possible. Even a single box turtle just 5 or 6 inches (12.5 or 15 cm) long feels cramped in a 4- x 8-foot (122 x 240-cm) enclosure and would use double that space. Most turtle enclosures are built in multiples of 8 feet because standard lumber sizes are in 8-foot (240-cm) increments. Enclosures

tend to be 8 x 8 feet (240 x 240 cm), 8 x 16 feet (240 x 480 cm), or 16 x 16 feet (480 x 480 cm).

To create a simple square or rectangular turtle pen, use 4-inch x 4-inch x 4-foot (10-cm x 10-cm x 122-cm) or 8-foot (240-cm) treated posts at the corners and at 8-foot (240-cm) intervals on longer sides. Bury the posts 12 to 18 inches (30 to 46 cm) into the ground for an enclosure that is sturdy enough to stop even giant tortoises. For the edges of the enclosure, use treated boards or outdoor plywood of a height of about 2 to 4 feet (61 to 122 cm), depending on whether you plan to add a gate or just step over the sides of the enclosure. Use galvanized nails or screws to attach the sideboards to prevent quick rusting. Remember that small turtles can climb well and will wedge themselves up corners. Affix 6-inch (15-cm) boards across the tops of the corners to keep turtles from going over and out. To prevent predators from jumping into the enclosure, place chicken wire or a similar light wire around the cage above the sideboards to a height of 2 or 3 feet (61 or 91 cm). Attach the wire loosely so it bows and flexes. The wire should be strong enough to prevent the entry of casual predators, such as a curious dog, but flexible enough to make it difficult or impossible for cats

The wire lid on this outdoor turtle cage helps keep out predators.

and rats to climb inside. If you have a serious problem with rats and cats climbing inside, you probably will have to fully wire the sides and top of the cage.

Underwiring

Most tortoise keepers quickly realize that a simple cage will not hold in a tortoise for very long if it has an urge to dig. This is especially true with African spurred or sulcata tortoises (*Geochelone sulcata*) and similar species that in nature dig deep burrows in which to spend the night. A small sulcata less than 2 feet (0.6 m) long can dig a burrow more than 6 feet (1.8 m) deep or long in a manner of hours, going under or through the bottom of a simple enclosure. To prevent this, underwire the entire floor of the enclosure with a fairly heavy welded wire with 1-inch (2.5-cm) spacing. Make sure the wire stretches from side to side of the enclosure and is cut to fit snugly around the upright supporting posts. Aluminum or plastic tent pegs allow you to quickly and safely fasten the wire into the ground. Few tortoises will attempt to dig through wire.

If the idea of underwiring doesn't appeal to you, you can insert a strip of metal (corrugated tin or sheet aluminum) at least a foot (30 cm) into the ground, leaving several inches above the ground completely around the perimeter of the enclosure. Tortoises will start to dig down, find that the barrier extends farther into the ground than they like, and stop to look for another spot to dig. Larger tortoises, of course, will need a barrier much deeper in the ground (possibly 3 feet [0.9 m]) to prevent escapes.

Sunken Cages

Some keepers and breeders of lizards such as tegus and plated lizards (*Gerrhosaurus* spp.) have found that these animals respond well to sunken cages. A sunken cage is a

Doghouses

Before building a retreat for a turtle or a tortoise or even a large lizard that doesn't especially like to climb, consider purchasing a doghouse instead. For a relatively low price, you can buy a premade heavy molded-plastic doghouse that will make a suitable night shelter for your pet and require no work on your part. Buy a model that is large enough for your pet, with (especially in the case of tortoises) a door wide enough to let it enter easily. Filled with a layer of hay, a doghouse (especially one with insulated walls) will keep a tortoise or a lizard comfortable on many nights from late spring through early autumn.

To install a heat lamp in your doghouse, buy a model with a separate roof that lifts off as a single piece and attaches to the body by tabs. Stretch a layer of half-inch (12.5-millimeter) hardware cloth across the entire top of the doghouse and anchor it into place with the roof. Cut a hole in the roof, place a low-wattage heat lamp inside, seal the opening with silicone cement, and run the electrical cord to a convenient outlet. The wire prevents hay or your pet from coming into contact with the lamp, which on a cool night can easily heat the doghouse ten or fifteen degrees Fahrenheit (about three to six degrees Celsius) above the outside temperature.

To build a sunken cage for turtles, a keeper inserted 3-foot sheets of metal into the ground.

very simple cage made by sinking a circle of sheet aluminum about 3 feet (91 cm) high roughly a foot (30 cm) into the ground, leaving 2 feet (61 cm) of wall aboveground around the enclosure. Rocks, soil, and lengths of PVC pipe to form burrows are added to the enclosure, and the lizards are allowed to just dig in. If the rocks are placed at the center of the enclosure, attempts to escape will be few and can be prevented by adding a couple of feet of chicken wire around the top edge. Many sunken cages are 6 to 8 feet (1.8 to 2.4 m) in diameter and can be used with large lizards. A sunken cage also works well for some turtles and tortoises that otherwise are difficult to maintain.

Place wire mesh over a sunken cage to keep out any predators.

Predators can easily jump over a 2-foot (61-cm) enclosure and wreak havoc among your pets. If you opt for a sunken cage, consider adding a cover such as lightweight corrugated plastic cut to fit the diameter of the enclosure and attached to thin lumber. During the winter, some breeders allow tegus to remain outdoors in sunken cages in protected areas by filling them with dead leaves and litter and then anchoring a tarpaulin over the cage to help hold in heat. Although sunken cages have lots of potential, they probably present more problems and hazards than they are worth.

Greenhouses

If you have a greenhouse already set up on your property, consider it as a year-round home for many types of lizards and turtles. It's also a great place to put almost any type of vivarium, from woodland to rain forest to desert, large or small. An existing greenhouse is not difficult to convert into a place to keep anything from frogs to uromastyx (*Uromastyx* spp.) to iguanas. There are, however, two problems with greenhouses: cost and escapes.

Unless you are planning to raise herps commercially, it is too expensive to build a greenhouse for general herp keeping. You will not only have to buy the materials or a kit and then pay to have the structure erected, but in many areas, you will also have to heat the greenhouse over much of the year. You will have to learn how to maintain the correct temperature and humidity within the greenhouse as well, which may require taking a course at a local college or consulting experienced gardeners in your area.

Making a greenhouse escape proof is difficult if you are not building it from scratch and including security measures in the construction. Double doors are essential if you keep fast lizards. There may be no way to let geckos such as day geckos (*Phelsuma* spp.) wander about the walls and ceilings because the movable ceiling panels used to adjust greenhouse temperatures are impossible to seal correctly for a small lizard. One option is to just place a large indoor vivarium in a greenhouse to give your pet access to natural sunlight and airflow it would never get inside your home.

A greenhouse is an excellent place to keep a vivarium.

Plants

Outdoor vivaria and cages give you lots of leeway when considering plants. It is quite possible to establish shrubs and flowering plants within an outdoor cage and let them grow normally. In dry areas, aloes, some cacti (such as spineless opuntia and pear cacti), and larger succulents may survive the warm part of the year but have to be taken indoors during the winter. In most areas, you can use shrubs of all types, including edible hibiscuses and even fruiting blueberries, as decorations that may survive fairly hard winters with just heavy mulching. Pots or beds of nasturtiums, violets, and similar edible plants will please many lizards and turtles.

Remember that it is larger herps that commonly are kept outdoors, and they will tend to trample any unprotected vegetation. Place wire cylinders around shrubs and other plantings, and keep flower beds out of the travel path of tortoises. Although sod provides an interesting background for many lizards and smaller turtles, tortoises tend to circle their enclosure endlessly, stopping occasionally to snack on random bits of vegetation. They will leave a packed trail behind after a few weeks that will not allow anything to grow.

If possible, talk with a knowledgeable person at your local nursery and explain your needs. Avoid plants known to be toxic to humans (although many of these are harmless

African violets make good plants for outdoor setups.

to reptiles), and try to buy native plants that will grow well in your area. Avoid purchasing expensive plants because you will probably have to replace them regularly. Potting plants may work much better than placing them in the ground. They will grow better and longer and allow you to remove the pot and plant to a protected area during the winter. As always, remember that gardening is a hobby separate from keeping herps—the animals deserve more of your attention than the plants do.

Hibiscus shrubs can be attractive additions to your vivarium—and they make a tasty snack for turtles.

CHAPTER 11

STERILE VIVARIA

I f you have a herp that is tolerant of sparse housing conditions, the sterile (or simple) vivarium will work for you. In this type of vivarium, everything is kept as simple as possible. The emphasis is on the animal rather than its surroundings. Sterile vivaria are not much to look at, but they work for more than half the herps you will find for sale and for almost any reptile coming from the eastern United States or Europe.

A sterile vivarium will safely hold your herp for the month it should be in quarantine before being added to your other animals or while it is being treated for a minor disease or parasite problem. It also is great for holding local herps for a few days or even weeks while they are being studied or photographed before returning them to the wild. (Remember that if you collect and release local herps, don't mix them with your other animals; keeping them separate reduces the chances of passing diseases and parasites between your stock.) Some large boas and pythons are kept in gigantic equivalents of sterile vivaria all their lives.

A basic sterile setup includes a newspaper substrate, a water bowl, and a hide box.

Basic Setup

The basic cage is usually a 20-gallon (76-liter) vivarium with a heavy metal mesh lid with a steel frame. However, almost any type of cage will work, including display units and those with sliding glass doors. This is not an especially wet setup, so the cage does not have to be extensively waterproofed. You will need a basking light for most herps, so be sure the lid can safely support one or that there are screened cutouts on the top or upper sides of the cage.

Many hobbyists prefer to use newspaper on the bottom of the sterile vivarium because it is cheap, is readily available, and can be easily replaced each day. A layer of coarse, unprinted newspaper stock at least three or four sheets thick looks clean and very scientific, whereas old papers look kind of sloppy. Be prepared to change all the papers each day, every day. To keep the vivarium clean, provide meals on a paper or plastic plate, and remove the plate after the meal is completed.

A sterile vivarium needs a good hide box because your animal will not have the luxury of moving around through branches and other backgrounds. The hide box can simply be an old cereal box with one end cut out or one of the types purchased from a pet supply shop. If you are keeping more than one animal in the vivarium, make sure that each has its own hide box.

You need a water bowl, preferably shallow and with a wide, heavy base, for most reptiles that don't come from hot desert conditions and for amphibians. You can keep amphibians in this type of vivarium, but maintaining a high relative humidity with just newspaper for bedding is difficult, requiring misting several times a day as well as a deeper water bath. Water baths tend to be messy, as the animals displace water each time they enter or leave, so the area around one is always soaking wet. Many herps will defecate in their water bowl if the bowl is large enough, so most keepers restrict the size of the bowl in a simple setup.

Most sterile vivaria work best for animals that are comfortable at room temperature most of the day and night— about 70°F to 80°F (21°C to 26.5°C) during the day, with a

drop of temperature at night by a few degrees. This means that a sterile vivarium depends on being in a warm room rather than on an undertank heater. Provide the cage with a weak basking light, such as an incandescent bulb of 20 to 40 watts in a conical metal holder situated out of reach of the herp. Place a flat slab of bark or a rock under the basking light. Note that many snakes and lizards do not really need to bask—this applies to almost any herp that is active mostly at night. They obtain most of their vitamin needs from their food and lots of their heat from residual heat in the soil and rocks. If you keep a frog or a corn snake, for instance, you don't need a basking light if the air and bedding temperatures stay relatively warm. A basking light is a luxury, but you may be surprised at how often snakes that "never bask" end up under the lamp for a few hours.

If you are keeping a young iguana or any other strong, diurnal basker in a sterile cage for a short period (such as during quarantine), you must provide it with a basking light. Almost any lizard that is active during the day and comes from a warm area (desert, open grasslands or prairie, edges of woodlands, openings in rain forests) needs a basking light.

Always give your herp a full-spectrum fluorescent light, even in the simplest vivarium and even if the animal is nocturnal. It is unknown how long a herp has to be exposed to sunlight to make sufficient vitamin D_3, but

seemingly nocturnal geckos bask briefly just as the sun goes up or down and produce a great amount of D_3 in just a few minutes. Some nocturnal herps get their D_3 from their food, but we know that just adding a D_3 supplement to food seldom increases the availability of the vitamin in the herp's bloodstream. A fluorescent full-spectrum light will not markedly increase the temperature and doesn't bother amphibians, so try to provide eight hours of full-spectrum light each day. Never forget to place at least one thermometer (preferably two) in the vivarium, one near the basking area or on the bedding and the other a bit higher up and in a cooler section.

A Note on Snake Drawer Units

Many woodland snakes from moderately cool areas and even some from the tropics do well without basking lights or high temperatures. They often are kept in simple drawer units, especially when they are breeding or raising young. Corn snakes, kingsnakes, and a number of smaller boas and pythons are among the many snakes that can spend their entire lives in drawer units. Drawer units are actually sterile vivaria that are furnished with either paper or a layer of aspen or pine shavings for bedding, a hide box (often just a cardboard paper towel tube for smaller snakes), and a water bowl. Although spartan, such surroundings suit many snakes very well, and they will thrive and breed in these conditions. Of course, you can't really display them, but you can house many snakes in a small area this way.

This is all you need to maintain a sterile vivarium. Sterile vivaria, however, are minimal vivaria. They don't give you much opportunity for individuality or making displays to show your friends. For this, you need to move on to a more sophisticated and complicated vivarium.

Quarantine

It makes sense to isolate any newly purchased herp from those you already have in your collection. This is especially true for wild-caught specimens of all groups, as they are very likely to be carrying parasites both externally (mites and ticks) and internally (intestinal worms and bacteria). Placing an infected herp in the same cage as a healthy one or even in an adjacent cage can quickly lead to infection of the healthy, established pet. Parasites and disease can be passed through contact with feces, skin secretions, and even bacteria transmitted through the air. The sterile vivarium makes a great quarantine cage.

Plan to hold any new purchase for at least a month and preferably six weeks in a sterile vivarium well away from your other pets. If possible, keep the quarantine vivarium in a separate room from the rest of your collection. A surprising number of wild-caught herps die within a few weeks of purchase or begin to show signs that they are ill, such as not feeding, loss of muscle tone, discoloration, or apathy.

This snake, like all newly acquired herps, should spend some time in quarantine before being introduced to the rest of the collection.

During the quarantine period, have all new purchases dewormed with an appropriate dewormer. Some products that are sold widely in pet supply shops, such as fenbendazole (Panacur), can be used to safely deworm many types of herps at home—but not all. Get a veterinarian's advice before trying to do it yourself. With more expensive or unusual herps, pay for a veterinary visit while the animal is in quarantine, and have the veterinarian pass on the health of the animal. Your veterinarian will be able to notice many problems that you may not see until too late. Often, these problems can be easily corrected.

After four to six weeks of quarantine, if the herp still appears healthy, is eating, and has been dewormed, you can add it to the general collection and perhaps move it into a more attractive decorated vivarium of the appropriate type.

Acclimation

The quarantine period in a sterile vivarium also represents your opportunity to acclimate a new pet to your keeping conditions. By keeping the new acquisition in a simple setup, you are able to give it more attention and see it more often. Be sure that every herp has an appropriate hiding place, whether a hide box, a plastic tray of litter and moss, or a length of cork bark under which to hide. Keep the vivarium relatively dark, but be sure to provide a basking lamp and undertank heating if needed. Disturb your new pet as little as possible as it adjusts to your presence and life in a relatively small habitat—as well as to new foods.

Many newly sold herps are dehydrated because the dealer was not able to give them sufficient water while they were on display. An important part of the acclimation process is to rehydrate the animal. This often can be done by assuring there is a fresh bowl of water in the vivarium at all times and making sure that the herp soaks at least twice a day in fresh water. Mist lizards such as chameleons twice a day. Always mist leaves or surfaces in their vivaria so they can lick water droplets. Some newly imported chameleons will rehydrate only if an automatic misting or fogging system is installed in the vivarium.

RESOURCES

Magazines

Reptiles
P.O. Box 6050
Mission Viejo, CA 92690
http://www.reptilesmagazine.com
A monthly magazine carrying articles on a wide variety of reptiles and amphibians and on vivaria. Articles by Rex Lee Searcey under the running title "The Living Vivarium" contain information on designing and building vivaria.

The Vivarium
Published from 1988 to 2000 by Philippe de Vosjoli, this was the first major herpetoculture magazine, and it contains many articles still of interest to all herp keepers. Back issues are available from Internet dealers and at reptile expos.

Books

Bartlett, R. D., and P. Bartlett. 1999. *Terrarium and Cage Construction and Care*. Hauppauge, NY; Barron's.

de Vosjoli, Philippe. 1996. *Design and Maintenance of Desert Vivaria: Step by Step Design, Enclosures, Hardware, Plants, Landscaping, Animals*. Irvine, CA: Advanced Vivarium Systems.

Ekarius, C. 2004. *How to Build Animal Housing*. North Adams, MA: Storey. Although the book is directed toward caging for farm animals, there are many good ideas here that could be used for small indoor and outdoor vivaria.

Walls, J. G. 1999. *The Guide to Plants for the Reptile Terrarium*. Neptune City, NJ: TFH.

INDEX

A

acclimation, 138
African bullfrogs (*Pyxicephalus*), 107
African spurred tortoises (*Geochelone sulcata*), 106, 116
African violets, 132
amphibians, 107, 134
anoles (*Sceloporus*), 93–94
antibacterial soaps, 87
aquariums, 6–11, 108–9
aquavariums, 108
artificial plants, 61–62, 93, 95–96, 105
aspen shavings, 36–37, 91, 92

B

backdrops, 44–46
bacteria, sphagnum moss for controlling, 110–11
bacterial contamination, 87, 88–89
bamboo, 43
basking behavior, 100, 101
basking lights, 68–69, 91–92, 96, 103, 135
basking perches, 39–43, 95
bathing tubs, 125
bedding. *See* substrates
begonias (*Begonia*), 52
bird's-nest ferns (*Asplenium*), 52–53
biting behaviors, 79–80
black and yellow tiger salamanders (*Ambystoma tigrinum*), 114
bleach for cleaning, 87–88
boas, 99, 102–3, 106, 124
box turtles (*Terrapene carolina*), 116, 125
branches, 39–43, 95
breeding large lizards, 121
bromeliads (*Tillandsia, Guzmania, Vriesea, Neoregelia,* and *Aechmea*), 53–54, 97
Burmese pythons (*Python molurus bivittatus*), 93
burrowing desert lizards, 103
buying herps: acclimation, 138; preparation for, 6; quarantine, 133, 137–38; wild-caught versus captive-bred, 105–6, 137

C

cables, heating, 74–75
cacti, 104
cages: about, 5–7; aquariums, 6–11, 108–9; cleaning, 87–89; for display, 17–18, 92; holding containers, 83, 87; for iguana, 19–20, 120–25, 135; indoor sunken, 130; laboratory cages, 16–17; mesh, 18–19, 97–98, 122; positioning, 22–24; snake drawers, 15–16, 136; for sterile vivaria, 134; tubs and shoe boxes, 12–15. *See also* do-it-yourself; vivaria
cannulas, 86
captive-bred herps, 106
carpet as substrate, 27–28
cast iron plants (*Aspidistra*), 54, 55
catheters, 86
cat litter, 33
cedar shavings, 37
Central American wood turtles (*Rhinoclemmys pulcherrima*), 116
ceramic heat emitter, 72
chameleons (*Chamaeleo*): dehydrated, 138; misting units for, 90, 93, 111, 138; vivaria for, 93–94
Chinese evergreens (*Aglaonema*), 54, 55–56
chuckwallas (*Sauromalus*), 105
cleaning tools, 87–89
climbing lizards, retreats for, 125
coconut husks, 34
combination lights, 70
common bearded dragon (*Pogona vitticeps*), 105
common kingsnakes (*Lampropeltis getula*), 106
cooling, 76–77
corn cobs, ground, 34
corn snakes (*Elaphe*), 93, 135
creeping fig (*Ficus pumila*), 56–57
cycle of desert herps, 100–101
cypress mulch, 35–36, 96

D

day geckos (*Phelsuma standingi*), 105, 130
daylight-white light, 67–68, 96–97

decorations. *See* landscaping and decorations; plants
dehydration, 138
desert gopher tortoises (*Gopherus agassizii*), 106
desert herps, 100–101, 105–7
desert iguanas (*Dipsosaurus*), 100, 102–3
desert racers (*Coluber*), 106
desert vivaria, 100, 101–5
deworming herps, 138
disease transmission, 137
display cages, 17–18, 92
doghouses, 128
do-it-yourself: cages, 20–22, 122–25, 128–30; food breeding, 6; greenhouse conversion, 130–31; turtle enclosures, 125–27, 129
doors, 93, 102, 119, 124
drain hole for wet vivaria, 111, 112
dusky salamanders (*Desmognathus*), 114

E
earless lizards (*Holbrookia*), 105–6
edible plants, 131
electronic thermometers, 91–92
emerald tree boas (*Corallus caninus*), 99
enclosures for turtles, 125–27, 129
equipment. *See* tools for herp keeping

F
fans, ventilating with, 110
feeding dishes, 47–48
feeding syringes, 85–87
fire salamanders (*Salamandra salamandra*), 114
fixed outdoor cages, 123–25
foggers, 89–90
footboards, 124
force feeding, 85–86
forceps, 84–85
frogs: bullfrogs, 107; poison, 108–9, 113, 114; in sterile vivaria, 135; and substrate, 111; tree frogs, 98, 99, 113
full-spectrum lighting, 63–65, 108, 109, 111, 135–36

G
geckos, 99
gopher tortoises (*Gopherus*), 106
gravel, 110
greenhouses, 130–31

green iguanas (*Iguana iguana*), 120–21
green tree pythons (*Python [Morelia] viridis*), 98, 99

H
handling snakes, 81
heating: about, 72–73; ceramic heat emitter, 72; heat rocks, 74, 75–76; safety considerations, 78; strips or cables, 74–75, 92; thermometers, 77–78, 91–92; undertank, 73–74, 92;
heat lamps, 125, 128
herpetoculture, 6
herpetology, 6
herps: definition of, 6; desert, 100–101, 105–7; outdoor, 117–20, 120–25, 128–30; rain forest, 98, 99; wet, 108–9, 113–14; wild-caught versus captive-bred, 105–6, 137; woodland, 93–94
hibiscuses, 131, 132
hide boxes, 46–47, 91, 92, 134
holding containers, 83, 87
hoods, lighting, 69
hooks, 79, 80–81
humidity, measuring, 78, 92–93, 103
hygrometers, 78, 92–93, 103

I
iguana cages, 19–20, 120–25, 135
iguanas, 100, 102–3, 120–21, 135

J
Jamaican anoles (*Sceloporus*), 94

L
laboratory cages, 16–17
landscaping and decorations: about, 38–39; backdrops, 44–46; branches, 39–43, 95; cleaning, 88–89; feeding dishes, 47–48; hide boxes, 46–47, 91, 92, 134; soaking tubs, 49–50; waterfalls, 98, 111–13. *See also* plants
leopard geckos (*Eublepharis macularius*), 105
leopard tortoises (*Geochelone pardalis*), 106, 116
lighting: about, 63; for basking, 68–69, 91–92, 96, 103, 135; combination, 70; full-spectrum, 63–65, 108, 109, 111, 135–36; normal, 67–68, 96–97;

and photoperiod, 70–72; for salamanders, 114; UVB, 66–67
lighting hoods, 69

M

mantellas (*Mantella*), 113
marbled salamanders (*Ambystoma opacum*), 114
mesh cages, 18–19, 97–98, 122
misters and misting, 89–90, 93, 97, 111, 138
monitors, large (*Varanus* spp.), 120–21
moss, 29–30, 110–11
movable outdoor cages, 121–22
mulch contaminants, 36
mulch substrates, 35–36, 96

N

nasturtiums, 131
newspaper, 26–27, 133, 134
normal white light, 67–68, 96–97
North American mole salamanders (*Ambystoma*), 114

O

ornamental figs (*Ficus*), 56–57
outdoor vivaria: doghouses for, 12; fixed, 123–25; greenhouses, 130–31; for large lizards, 120–25, 128–30; movable, 121–22; overview, 115–17; plants for, 131–32; for small lizards, 117–20; sunken cages, 128–30; turtle enclosures, 125–27

P

paper, reprocessed, 34
parasite transmission, 137
philodendrons (*Philodendron*), 57, 59
photoperiod considerations, 70–72
pine shavings, 36–37
plants: about, 50–51; artificial, 61–62, 93, 95–96, 105; begonias, 52; bird's-nest ferns, 52–53; bromeliads, 53–54, 97; cast iron plants, 54, 55; Chinese evergreens, 54, 55–56; edible, 131; ornamental figs, 56–57; philodendrons and pothos, 57, 59, 111; prayer plants, 58, 59; snake plants, 58, 59–60, 105; succulents, 60–61, 104–5, 131
plastic sheeting, 110

poison dart frogs (*Dendrobates*), 108–9, 113, 114
poison frogs (*Epipedobates and Phyllobates*), 113
positioning cages, 22–24
pothos (*Scindapsus*), 57, 59, 111
potted plants, 132
prayer plants (*Maranta*), 58, 59
predators and outdoor cages, 122, 126–27, 130
pythons (*Python*), 93, 98, 99

Q

quarantine, 133, 137–38

R

racerunners (*Cnemidophorus*), 105–6
rain forest herps, 98, 99
rain forest vivaria, 95–98, 111–13
rat snakes (*Elaphe*), 93
razor blades, cleaning with, 88
red-eared sliders (*Trachemys scripta elegans*), 108
red-eyed tree frogs (Agalychnis callidryas), 98, 99
Reptiles (magazine), 6
retreats for large lizard cages, 125, 128
rheostats, 75
rock iguanas (*Cyclura* spp.), 120–21
rocks: for climbing, 104; for heating, 74, 75–76; as substrate, 32–33
rosy boas (*Lichanura trivirgata*), 106
rubber plants (*Ficus elastica*), 56–57

S

safety considerations: cleaning cages, 87, 88–89; and container contents, 89; handling herps, 79–84; for heating, 78
salamanders, 113–14
sand, 30–32, 101–2
sand boas (*Eryx*), 102–3, 106
shields, 83–84
shoe boxes as cages, 12–15
shrubs, 131
simple vivaria, 133–38
small lizard outdoor vivaria, 117–20
snake drawer units, 15–16, 136
snake handling, 81

snake hooks, 79, 80–81
snake plants (*Sansevieria*), 58, 59–60, 105
snake tongs, 82
soaking tubs, 49–50
soaps, warning about, 87
spadefoot toads (*Scaphiopus*), 107
Spanish moss (*Tillandsia usneoides*), 53
sphagnum moss, 29–30, 110–11
spiny-tailed iguanas (*Ctenosaura* spp.), 120–21
spiny-tailed lizards (*Uromastyx*), 100, 105
spot cleaning, 89
spotted salamanders (*Ambystoma maculatum*), 114
sterile vivaria, 133–38
strips, heating, 74–75, 92
substrates: about, 25–26; aspen shavings, 36–37, 91, 92; carpet, 27–28; cleaning, 89, 111; gravel, 110; moss, 29–30, 110–11; mulch, 35–36, 96; newspaper, 26–27, 133, 134; nontraditional, 33–34; pine shavings, 36–37; rocks, 32–33; sand, 30–32, 101–2
succulents (*Euphorbia, Gasteria,* and *Haworthia*), 60–61, 104–5, 131
sunken cages, 128–30
sunlight, 67–68, 101, 125
swifts (*Sceloporus*), 93, 105–6
syringes, 85–86, 87

T
tegus (*Tupinambis* spp.), 120–21, 128
temperature: cooling, 76–77; outdoors, 116; thermometers, 77–78, 91–92. *See also* heating
Texas gopher tortoises (*Gopherus berlandieri*), 106
thermometers, about, 77–78, 91–92
tiger salamanders (*Ambystoma tigrinum*), 114
timers, 71–72, 103
toads (*Bufo*), 107
tongs, 82
tools for herp keeping: about, 79, 90; cleaning, 87–89; forceps, 84–85; medical tools, 85–87; misters and foggers, 89–90, 93,
111, 138; misting systems, 97, 111; safety-oriented, 79–84; shields, 83–84; snake hooks, 79, 80–81; snake tongs, 82. *See also* heating; lighting
tortoises, 106, 115, 116, 125–28
tree frogs, 98, 99, 113
tropical day geckos (*Phelsuma*), 99
tropical tree frogs (*Hyla*), 99
tubs as cages, 12–15
tubs for soaking, 49–50
turtle enclosures, 115, 125–27, 129
turtles, 115, 116, 125–27, 129

U
UL label, 78
undertank heaters, 73–74, 92
underwiring for tortoise enclosures, 127–28
uromastyx (*Uromastyx* spp.), 105, 130
UVB lights, 66–67

V
veterinarians: for deworming, 138; for force feeding, 85–86
vinegar for cleaning, 87–88
violets, 131
vitamin D3, 135–36
vivaria: about, 4–6; desert, 100, 101–5; rain forest, 95–99, 111–13; sterile, 133–38; wet, 108–13; woodland, 91–94. *See also* cages; outdoor vivaria

W
walnut shells, ground, 33, 34
water baths, 112
water bowls, 102, 133, 134
waterfalls, 98, 111–13
water monitors (*Varanus salvator*), 123
weeping fig plants (*Ficus benjamina*), 56–57
wet vivaria, 108–13
wet vivaria herps, 108–9, 113–14
whipsnakes (*Masticophis*), 106
wild-caught herps, 105–6, 137
Wolterstorff, Willy, 4
woodland herps, 93–94
woodland vivaria, 91–93

Z
zoning laws, 123

ABOUT THE AUTHOR

A native of central Louisiana, **Jerry Walls** has always been interested in animals and plants. After obtaining an M.S. degree in biology from McNeese in Lake Charles (with a thesis on the taxonomy of several southern crawfishes), he moved to New Jersey and began work as an editor for TFH Publications. During the thirty years he was with TFH, he authored more than 400 publications on a variety of natural history subjects, including recent work on reptiles and amphibians. Among these publications are more than forty books, ranging from introductory works on lizards and turtles as pets to massive reviews of seashells. His more than twenty books on reptiles and amphibians and his editorship of the magazine *Reptile Hobbyist* have helped make him one of the better-known names in the field of terrarium pets. He also has written the monthly breeder's column in *Reptiles* magazine.

An active birder with more than 600 species on his life-list, Jerry enjoys roaming the field when time permits, looking for interesting animals and plants for his wife, Maleta, to photograph and to serve as the topics for new articles. He and Maleta live in central Louisiana on twelve acres, with five dogs, numerous cats, several snakes and turtles, and assorted rodents.